THE
LAND & PEOPLE
JESUS KNEW

THE LAND & PEOPLE JESUS KNEW

A Visual Tour of First-Century Palestine
Written & Illustrated by

J. ROBERT TERINGO

BETHANY HOUSE PUBLISHERS
MINNEAPOLIS, MINNESOTA 55438

The paper used in this book meets the minimum requirements of the American National Standard for Permanence of Paper for Printed Library Materials, Z39.48-1984.

THE LAND & PEOPLE JESUS KNEW

Published by Bethany House Publishers
A Division of Bethany Fellowship, Inc.
6820 Auto Club Road, Minneapolis, MN 55438

Printed in the United States of America

Library of Congress Cataloging-in-Publication Data

Teringo, J. Robert.
   The land and people Jesus knew.

   Bibliography: p.
   Includes index.
   1. Palestine — Description and travel — Views.
2. Bible — Illustrations. 3. Palestine — Antiquities.
4. Palestine — Social life and customs — To 70 A.D.
5. Bible — Antiquities. 6. Jews — Antiquities
7. Jews — Social life and customs — To 70 A.D.
I.   Title.
DS108.5.T47   1985   220.9'1   85-13550
ISBN 0-87123-797-0

To Dorothy

Because of your support,
encouragement and dedicated assistance,
this book has become a reality.

I am greatly indebted to the following scholars for their expert advice and assistance:

Dr. Barry M. Gittlen, professor of archeology at Baltimore Hebrew College, my project consultant and advisor; *Dr. Lionel Casson*, for assistance in reconstructing the fishing boats and gear, as well as the Roman ships; *Dr. Joseph Baumgarten*, also of Baltimore Hebrew College, for guidance in portraying first-century Judaism; *Dr. William L. MacDonald*, for expert advice on Roman architecture and the architecture of first-century Jerusalem; *Dr. Betty Jo Mayeske*, for the dress of the Romans and the Roman army; *Dr. Robert L. Hohlfelder*, University of Colorado, for assisting in reconstructing the harbor of Caesarea; and *Frederick D. Phillips*, my editor, for guiding my words.

A very special thanks to my wife, Dorothy, for her seemingly endless task of typing and re-typing the manuscript.

CONTENTS

INTRODUCTION

The historical existence of Jesus of Nazareth is a fact, as much a fact as that of any person in biblical history. We know of him, not through his own writings, as none exist; nor from monuments of the period to his glory, as none were built; nor from stone reliefs, as none were carved; but, through the written documents and letters of his contemporaries, men of his own time. These ancient authors tell us Jesus was a Jew who lived in a definite time period and in a definite place, a region we can find on today's maps.

Reading these writings makes us acutely aware that these are Oriental books, written in another age by Easterners and for Easterners, about Eastern people and events. As we read on, those of us from a Western culture begin to realize the importance of interpreting these words from the proper viewpoint, one based on a knowledge of the times, its people, and their manners and customs. This kind of interpretation provides the clearest understanding of the lessons, stories, and parables of these great writings.

This, then, is the basic purpose of *The Land and People Jesus Knew*: to bring to life as many aspects of daily life as possible, and bring them to life in accurate, informative visuals. I purposed, therefore, to find, organize, and then visualize, vast amounts of detailed information until every aspect of first-century life was dealt with.

With these goals in mind, I determined to avoid the inaccuracies and inconsistencies of most daily-life books and art of a biblical nature. I strived to produce a biblical visual that shows a deep feeling and concern for the subject matter, yet is accurately researched and presented in an exciting, interesting way.

This book, therefore, is not intended to document or illustrate the life or work of Jesus, or expound a creed or doctrine, but simply to reconstruct, as accurately as data permits, the world of Jesus and his contemporaries — a world they saw as they traveled about first-century Palestine.

The idea for *The Land and People Jesus Knew* grew from simple questions, asked by inquiring minds about the life in Palestine. These typical Sunday school students could find only limited, and often incorrect, data. My desire for information developed into a project that required eight years of intense study and drawing, and three extensive research trips to Bible lands.

The Land and People Jesus Knew was a labor of love. Though the book covers a brief period (approximately 5–6 B.C. to A.D. 70), it became a research and art project of enormous complexity and proportions. The greatest portion of the information required came from original sources: the New Testament itself and the works of the great Jewish historian Flavius Josephus. The principal source, the Gospels, deals mainly with Jesus and the life around him, while Josephus (in addition to recording the history of the Jews leading up to and following after Jesus' time) gives detailed information of life in the first century A.D. The Talmud, another important source, comprises a collection of many Jewish laws and traditions pertaining to daily life. Other ancient authors, and modern books, studies and articles (check the Bibliography for selected sources) provide insights and newly acquired information on the times. In addition, biblical archeologists contribute a growing mass of relevant data from new sites, including artifacts, coins, etc.

To insure accuracy, a biblical scholar reviewed and verified the data and interpretations, and scrutinized the text and the details in the art. Other experts helped resolve specific problems with data, or the lack of it, and guided the development of reconstruction. Their expertise has enabled some aspects of daily life to be presented for the first time. In addition, my extensive work with scholars in developing historical art reconstruction for the *National Geographic Magazine,* along with the availability of some unique research materials, aided my quest for accuracy and detail.

Here is an example of the labor required to produce some of the visuals: I needed to determine the shape, size and construction of the boats used on the Sea of Galilee by fishermen such as Simon Peter and his brother, Andrew. This problem had interested me for some time, but my research produced very little data. When I was finally faced with developing the reconstruction drawings, I discussed my concerns with a leading authority on ancient ships and their construction. Many drawings followed his extensive research before realistic reconstructions were developed, based upon data assimilated from ancient texts, mosaics, and reliefs of boats from the same period. To my knowledge such reconstructions, as many others in this book, have never been as thoroughly researched and developed into visuals as those on the following pages.

To present a comprehensive picture of life in *The Land and People Jesus Knew*, we shall begin with the setting itself, Palestine. Many major biblical events took place on this small stage. Palestine proper was made up of large, Greek-dominated urban centers, and hundreds of widely scattered small towns and villages. The villages consisted mostly of common people, many working as farmers. We will look closely at their houses, structures of simple stone and mud brick, and will also see how they dressed and adorned themselves.

Work, the way the people earned their daily bread, comprised a big part of everyday life, just as it does today. We will look closely at where the people worked, what tools they used, and how each person's work was seen by others. We will observe the legendary life of the shepherd and the other noble occupations that touched the lives of nearly everyone, such as the carpenter, the potter and the fisherman. These, along with the farmer, were significant and were constantly mentioned in biblical stories and parables.

Then we will look at the Chosen People and how the Jews responded to their special covenant. We need to know what was in their hearts and minds as they lived amidst their network of customs and traditions that directed every aspect of their lives. We shall also visit Jerusalem with all its splendor and grandeur, the sacred stronghold of Judaism, the city Jesus knew well.

With Palestine situated at the great crossroads of the ancient trade routes, trade and commerce were always an important part of daily life. But, Palestine was an occupied country, and its Jewish population felt the oppression of Rome and the strong influences of the Greco-Roman culture.

As this book concept developed, various uses became apparent. Bible students using *The Land and People Jesus Knew* will find its material unbiased and relevant to an understanding of this specific period in Bible history. Teachers will find the visuals add interest and excitement to the learning experience. Bible scholars will find the coverage comprehensive, accurate, and current with the discoveries of biblical archeology. Families will find New Testament times "coming alive" if *The Land and People Jesus Knew* is kept handy for study and discussion; as a "coffee table" book its availability for browsing and casual study will help sustain interest in Bible times.

The uses are as endless as the numbers of its readers and their needs. Most readers are likely to find hundreds of opportunities to refer to and use this valuable aid for a better understanding of *The Land and People Jesus Knew*.

J. Robert Teringo

CHAPTER·ONE

THE LAND OF THE BOOK

At the extreme southwestern edge of Asia on the shores of the Mediterranean Sea, we find a land of great scenic diversity and beauty. Palestine is small by most geographic standards. It, however, stands as a giant because of its remarkable history of extraordinary events. Appropriately we begin our first-century visit with an overview of the land Jesus knew and loved.

Palestine occupied only a small portion of the greater frontier province of Syria, Rome's easternmost province, which extended from Asia Minor in the north, to the great Arabian Desert in the south. Palestine, on Syria's western border, stood at the very crossroads of Asia and Africa. Positioned between the sea on the west and the desert on the east, it provided a bridge between the great civilizations of Asia and Egypt, offering a traveler or caravan as many as five major highways to choose from. Palestine was under the direct control and authority of the Syrian governor, who was under the ultimate rule of Rome.

This narrow, coastal bridge is harshly interrupted by two great mountain ranges running north and south for its full length. These mountains sit on each side of the great Jordan Valley rift, with only a few open plains interposing this continuous chain. Along with the coastal plain, these were always cultivated to their fullest extent; for few broad, fertile areas were available to produce the grain necessary to feed a growing population. Unfortunately, much of southern Palestine was bleak wilderness, with few tillable acres.

Throughout the first century, plants and animals played an integral role in the daily life of the people. The plants fueled the fires and supplied food for the tables, while the trees provided fresh fruit as well as much-needed shade from the hot summer sun. The fields of wildflowers offered a beauty unsurpassed in all Southwest Asia. Domesticated animals provided not only meat, wool, milk, and leather, but power as well. Animals pulled the plows across the fields of Palestine and helped to carry the burdens of those heavily laden peasants. Birds abounded, and the sea and rivers teemed with fish of all kinds, while the common insects helped make life uncomfortable even in those ancient days.

Palestine was composed of three main districts: Judea, Samaria and Galilee. We shall first explore the district of Judea. Approximately fifty miles from north to south and only twenty-five miles wide, its area was small, yet it was the largest district in first-century Palestine. Judea lay at the southern frontier of Palestine, reaching to Idumea and the desert of Arabia. On the north it shared a boundary with the district of Samaria. To the east Judea's boundary was the winding lower Jordan River and almost the entire length of the Dead Sea. The coastal country of Philistia lay to the west, while further north was the vast Mediterranean Sea. The most famous district in Palestine, Judea became an independent Roman province in A.D. 6, with its governor, the Procurator, reporting directly to Rome.

Much of the diverse landscape of Judea had a rugged beauty, as off-white limestone jutted up from the bleak soil. Throughout the district, parched and untilled countryside rose abruptly to meet man-made stone terraces that clung to the barren hills. The trees and vines growing on these narrow terraces appeared as ribbons of green on dull, reddish-brown slopes.

Not all Judea was barren and bleak,

however. In the first century one could see acres of golden wheat, countless groves of silver-green olive trees, and bright, colorful carpets of winter flora. The hardy grape vine, with its deep purple fruit basking in the sun under the blue sky, formed a patchwork of color on the Judean landscape.

Through the center of this parched countryside ran a mountainous spine that dropped sharply to the maritime plain on the Mediterranean; to the east, the dry, featureless plateau overlooked the Jordan Valley. As one reached the desolate wilderness on the east, the limited areas of cultivation quickly changed to rolling, rocky hills, sparsely covered with dry, brown grass. Hundreds of deep ravines, or *wadis*, cut sharply through the crumbling sandstone and barren soil. This was the very wilderness where John the Baptist preached, and Jesus prepared for his ministry.

Judea was not only the home of a proud and passionate people with deep religious feelings, but the arena for many great historical and religious events. A Jewish state, with Jerusalem as both its political capital and the seat of Jewish religious authority, Judea provided the center of worship—the great second temple. In Judea we find the site of Jesus' birth, the place of much of his ministry, and Jerusalem, the site of his death. From the outside, first-century Jerusalem gave the impression of a strong, impregnable city with a stout outer wall and gigantic buildings, while within, wall followed upon wall. The eyes of Palestine, as well as those of the entire Jewish world, focused on Judea and, in particular, Jerusalem and its temple.

At the geographic center of Palestine lay the small district of Samaria. Enclosed between Judea on the south, Galilee on the north, and Peraea on the east, Samaria was the smallest of the three districts that made up Palestine proper. Early in the first century, Samaria became part of Judea under the Roman Procurator, but never really gave up its identity. As part of the hill country a rock spine ran through the center of its entire length. Many of the ancient roads to the heart of Palestine crisscrossed these mountains.

In Samaria we would have found the largest man-made harbor in the Roman world, constructed at the Greek city of Caesarea, the new center of sea trade and commerce for Palestine. When it became the home for the Roman Procurator, Caesarea became the Roman political capital of Judea and Samaria.

Although the Roman authorities politically combined the districts of Judea and Samaria, Judeans and Samaritans never recognized the union. Hatred between these groups dated back to the Judeans' return from exile in 538 B.C. By the first century A.D. this hatred was so intense that a Jewish pilgrim passing through Samaria to or from Jerusalem placed himself in great danger.

When Herod the Great died in 4 B.C., his son Archelaus inherited Judea, Samaria, and Idumea. Archelaus, however, was deposed after only a short reign, and in A.D. 6 his territory was placed under the governorship of a Roman Procurator. The hatred between Jew and Samaritan, however, prevented any hope of unity in the upcoming Roman onslaught.

The northern district of Palestine, Galilee, a small but important area of great fertility and genial climate, was a land of beauty. Between the Mediterranean Sea and Galilee's western border stood the country of Phoenicia, while the Jordan River and the Sea of Galilee defined the district's eastern border. In the north, rugged mountains divided it from Syria, while the great plain of Esdraelon in the south separated Galilee from the middle district of Samaria. Extending approximately fifty miles from north to south, and only thirty miles east to west, Galilee was divided into two main geographical areas—northern or Upper Galilee and the southern "Galilee of the nations." Everywhere in Galilee one would have seen the expansive natural beauty of forest-covered mountains, broad fertile valleys, and vast areas of cultivated fields. Terraced hillsides dominated the steeper slopes, while lush vegetation and an abundance of multi-colored wildflowers gave a bright finishing touch.

At the time of Jesus' ministry, Lower Galilee contained a diverse population, including a large number of Jews. Villages and towns crowded the valleys and ringed the shoreline along the deep expanse of the Sea of Galilee. The extensive commerce and industry in these towns, especially the grain and fishing industries, were the very lifeblood of the region. The men of Galilee proved themselves an industrious lot whose nature demanded an intense, outdoor life. The gentle disciple, as well as the wild, fanatical zealot, came from these hardy people.

Most Galileans were especially devoted to their religion and extremely patriotic to their homeland, yet they were disdained by the more orthodox Jews of Judea, especially those from Jerusalem. Partly because of this attitude, pious Jews did not expect, or even imagine, that anyone of importance could come from such a lowly group so far from great Jerusalem. Yet to these very men of Galilee new ideas and teachings of Jesus had great appeal and were readily accepted.

In the world of first-century Palestine, the many neighboring nations with their varied cultures played a significant role in the daily life of the people of Judea, Samaria, and Galilee. The largest and most important neighbor, Syria, from which the Romans administered Palestine, extended from the Euphrates River in the north, to the great Arabian Desert just beyond Judea's border. A frontier province, it served as an important buffer zone on the empire's eastern flank. The glory of Syria was not just in its status with Rome, but in its magnificent forests of cedar. The huge "cedars of Lebanon" produced a wood so beautiful that it was employed solely for the decoration of important buildings.

North of Galilee and next to Syria, we would have found Phoenicia, one of the greatest maritime nations in the ancient world. Beyond the headlands of Mount Carmel, Phoenicia lay as a narrow strip between Syria and the Mediterranean Sea.

Continuing clockwise from Phoenicia, we would enter the lands of the great Decapolis. This territory belonged to a federation of ten Greek cities which had banded together for commercial and cultural reasons. For the people of Palestine they were influential neighbors with a strong pagan culture.

Peraea was a desolate wilderness paralleling the Jordan Valley to the Dead Sea. Although east of the Jordan River, it was considered Jewish land with its few inhabitants living in small settlements of Jews and bands of shepherding Arab nomads. Traveling pilgrims used Peraea to bypass Samaria on their way to or from Jerusalem.

The frontier south of Palestine included Philistia on the coast, and the land of Idumea inland. Idumea, the western extension of ancient Edom, reached south to the great desert of Arabia. Shortly before the first century Idumeans converted to Judaism and united with Judea, thereby becoming part of Palestine proper.

The political geography changed frequently in Palestine, and by the first century a Hellenistic spirit was sweeping across all of southwest Asia. Greek culture and architecture embellished the land everywhere as the Roman rulers actively promoted this pagan culture and its religion.

The environment, its people and animals, and the complex political and cultural factors, all played their parts in setting the stage for a new series of events in the long history of Palestine. Unknown to the peoples of this land and time, however, events were unfolding, destined to live in the hearts and minds of men, women, and children of the next two thousand years.

■

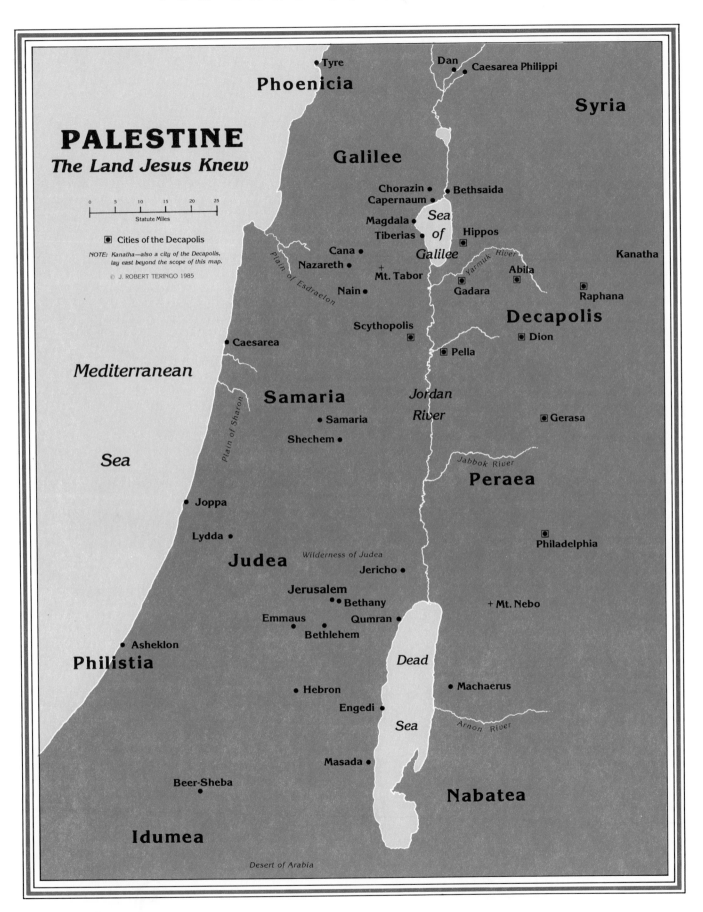

PALESTINE
The Land Jesus Knew

0   5   10   15   20   25
Statute Miles

◉ Cities of the Decapolis

NOTE: Kanatha—also a city of the Decapolis,
lay east beyond the scope of this map.

© J. ROBERT TERINGO 1985

Phoenicia

• Tyre

Dan

• Caesarea Philippi

Syria

Galilee

Chorazin •   • Bethsaida
Capernaum •

Magdala •   Sea
Tiberias •   of
Galilee

Hippos ◉

Kanatha

Cana •

Nazareth •

Yarmuk River

Abila ◉

+
Mt. Tabor

Nain •

Gadara ◉

Raphana ◉

Plain of Esdraelon

Decapolis

Scythopolis
◉

Dion ◉

Caesarea •

◉ Pella

Mediterranean

Samaria

Jordan

Samaria •

River

Gerasa ◉

Shechem •

Sea

Jabbok River

Plain of Sharon

Peraea

Joppa •

Lydda •

Philadelphia ◉

Judea   Wilderness of Judea

Jericho •

Jerusalem
•• Bethany
Emmaus •   Qumran •
Bethlehem •

+ Mt. Nebo

• Asheklon

Dead

Philistia

• Hebron

• Machaerus

Engedi •

Sea

Arnon River

Masada •

Nabatea

Beer-Sheba
•

Idumea

Desert of Arabia

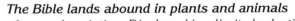

The Bible lands abound in plants and animals
of every description. Displayed is a limited selection
of the flora and fauna to be seen in this diverse
land: (1) sheep, (2) ox, (3) camel, (4) goat,
(5) leopard, (6) donkey, (7) bee, (8) mosquito,
(9) camel fly, (10) turtledove, (11) pigeon,
(12) scorpion, (13) flax, (14) fox, (15) wolf,
(16) lilies of the field, (17) mustard, (18) thistle,
(19) eagle, (20) cock, (21) owl, (22) fig palm,
(23) olive tree, (24) viper.

The small village of Bethany is situated on the east slopes of the Mount of Olives, along the road from Jerusalem to Jericho. The village was surrounded by green terraces and groves of olive trees, and was often a place to lodge overnight for those visiting overcrowded Jerusalem. Bethany was also the home of Lazarus, Mary, and Martha, close friends of Jesus.

The Dead Sea fills the deepest part of the Jordan Valley depression, with no outlet. Its surface is 1,290 feet below sea level. When seen from a distance it appears an intense blue, beautiful in its barren setting. Up close, the water being evaporated by intense sunlight gives off an offensive odor and leaves a salt content so high no living thing can survive in the sea.

The wilderness of Judea lies between Jerusalem and the Dead Sea. It is a rocky and barren tract with an endless succession of dull-colored hills void of grass and trees, and with few centers, i.e., Jericho, Masada, Qumran and Engedi. These barren and rocky hills were inhabited mainly by nomads pasturing their sheep and goats. This wilderness was also the setting for Jesus' temptation, and was a lurking place for thieves who preyed upon traveling pilgrims and merchants.

The Rock of Masada

The rock of Masada stands in majestic isolation overlooking the Dead Sea. Because its remoteness, savage height, and precipitous sides provided a fortress unmatched in natural strength, Herod richly furnished the plateau with a multi-level palace, storehouses, barracks, water cisterns and fortifications. Masada was the site of a dramatic first-century struggle between the Jewish Zealots and the 10th Legion of Rome.

Bethlehem lies in a fertile area in the central chain of Judea's mountains five or six miles south of Jerusalem. Below the thriving hillside town, ripening grain lent its golden color to the fields, and vineyards grew on rocky slopes. In outlying areas stood natural caves in the limestone rock, which were often used as temporary shelter by men or beasts.

The lush Mount of Olives sits on the east side of the Kidron Valley opposite Jerusalem. The mount, with its beautiful gardens and olive groves, stands as the last great ridge before the long descent into the Jordan Valley. In Jesus' time the southeastern part of this mount was the traditional Jewish burial ground.

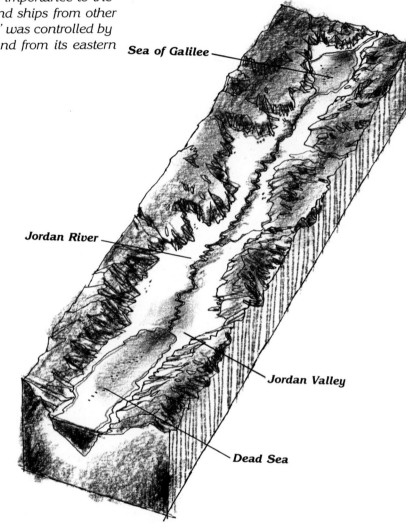

The Mediterranean Sea was the commercial gateway to the Roman world. Although foreign trade was of considerable importance to the Jewish merchants, they preferred to hire sailors and ships from other nations for their maritime ventures. The "great sea" was controlled by Rome and carried Rome's grain and soldiers to and from its eastern provinces.

Sea of Galilee

Jordan River

Jordan Valley

Dead Sea

The flourishing city of Sebaste was the old city of Samaria which had been rebuilt and renamed shortly before the first century. It boasted a great colonnade and magnificent Greek and Roman style buildings. The city, inhabited mainly by Gentiles, soon became a center for Greek culture and influence, and the political capital of the district of Samaria.

The great Jordan Valley contains the only river in Palestine of any size. The Jordan River begins its life as fresh, clear water from the mountains of Lebanon, pursues its winding course to the Sea of Galilee, and then flows on to the Dead Sea. Shut in by steep cliffs the river zigzags, making a path two hundred miles long through a valley stretching only sixty-five miles between the two seas. The water descends one thousand feet through dozens of falls and rapids to its lowest depth—the Dead Sea. Here the life of the Jordan River abruptly ends.

Jacob's well provided a place to stop when traveling the great road through the district of Samaria. Traditionally situated near biblical Shechem, the well lay at a main fork, whose one branch led to the new capital, Sebaste, the other to nearby towns.

At the sea entrance to Caesarea's harbor, massive towers and lighthouse greeted incoming sailors with their first view of Palestine. Herod built this massive seaport entirely of marble and white-plastered stone, and adorned it with temples, a palace and public buildings of great splendor. His greatest work, however, was the harbor itself, with breakwater walls extending into the open sea that were large enough to include towers, buildings and docks. As the home of the Roman Procurator, Caesarea became the Roman political capital of Judea and Samaria, and the gateway to Rome.

The new city of Tiberias was situated on the west shore of the Sea of Galilee. Herod Antipas built this walled city to serve as his capital and named it in honor of Emperor Tiberius. No pious Jew would set foot in this city built on an old cemetery site; it was populated, therefore, by heathens and the scum of Herod's kingdom.

Nazareth rests in a hilltop basin that today seems to shut out the outside world. In the first century, however, Nazareth juxtaposed busy ancient roads on which pilgrims thronged to and from Jerusalem, and merchant caravans passed through almost daily from Egypt or Damascus. The villagers of Nazareth observed and felt the influences of the outside world.

The Sea of Galilee, with its beautiful grey-blue water, was the focus of northern Palestine. On its waters fleets of fishing boats were visible, and in its depths, fish abounded. At the time of Jesus' ministry Galilee's shores were the most populated rural area in all Palestine. It was in the environs of the Sea of Galilee that Jesus spent much of his public life.

The great roads were an important feature of Galilee. This northern region was crisscrossed by ancient highways that led from the sea to the desert, and from Egypt to Syria. People quipped that "Judea is on the road to nowhere—Galilee is covered with roads to everywhere."

The crescent-shaped plain of Gennesaret extends along the western shore of the sea. Admired for its beauty and rich soil, it was a virtual garden of Eden, where many varieties of crops were cultivated.

Capernaum was the center of Jesus' ministry and the site of a synagogue built by a Roman centurion. This important fishing town on the north shore of the Sea of Galilee was situated on the "high road," a trade route between Egypt and Syria. As a major customs center, Capernaum housed a Roman garrison to enforce the collection of duties.

Peraea, the "region beyond," was a vast wilderness area that extended east from the Jordan River to the Syrian desert. Jews formed the bulk of the population, while small bands of Arabs wandered in the desert areas. The Jews regarded Peraea, along with Galilee and Judea, as one of the three Jewish provinces. When pilgrims trekked south to Jerusalem by way of Peraea, to bypass Samaria, they considered their journey traveled wholly on Jewish soil.

The Decapolis was a famous first-century confederation of ten Greek cities near the heart of Palestine. The cities, built in the Greek and Roman style of architecture, featured colonnaded streets, great roads and bridges, amphitheaters, baths, temples, gates, and other magnificent private and public structures.

The Decapolis comprised ten cities. Scholars agree on eight: Hippos, Gadara, Raphana, Pella, Dion, Gerasa, Philadelphia, and Scythopolis (the only member city west of the Jordan River). Scholars are divided as to which cities made up the other two. Those cities were Damascus, Kanatha, and Abila. The confederation was organized for commercial and cultural reasons, as well as a means to preserve and promote the Hellenistic spirit in a predominantly Jewish territory.

Idumea lay in the southern part of Palestine, between Judea and the great Arabian desert. This southern frontier transformed, almost without notice, from pasture land between parched hills, to the desolate desert of Sinai. Idumea was a land of caves where hermits settled and fugitives from Greek cities took refuge.

Phoenicia, the great maritime nation of the ancient world, lay north of Palestine on a narrow strip between the mountains and the sea. Iron anchors of this type were used by Phoenician sailors. Merchants and seamen rather than agricultural people, the Phoenicians could be found in ports throughout the Mediterranean world.

C H A P T E R · T W O

LIFE IN TOWN AND COUNTRY

Year after year, tents were set on the grassy hillside near a spring of clear, cold water. As time passed permanent dwellings began to appear and, as has happened throughout history, the cluster of primitive huts grew into a village. The inhabitants soon found it necessary to call themselves by a collective name—"the village of so and so."

As a town grew and prospered, more of the surrounding countryside came under its cultivation or was used for pasturing the growing flocks. As they continued to prosper, the residents felt increasingly vulnerable, so as soon as possible they began to fortify.

Early civilizations set the example. They surrounded their settlements with large ditches and planted stout hedges on the inside. Often within these enclosures a simple watchtower or scaffolding was constructed to give a vantage point and, if the need occurred, to provide a place from which to fight off invaders. So developed the art of city fortification.

First-century Palestine benefited from this developing technology. As many of its towns and cities built modern fortifications, some developed their defenses to the point where their towns were considered impregnable. Only the important urban centers were enclosed by walls, as fortifications were extremely expensive, difficult to build, and took years to complete. In times of crisis the smaller neighboring towns and villages depended totally upon the walled cities for refuge and protection. The dependent villages and towns would, as the price for refuge, provide men and arms to help protect the city if it came under attack.

Size, however, was not the only factor for determining if a city should be fortified. The elevation of a city, its natural barriers, and the adequacy of its water supply were important considerations. Major centers of trade, or cities that would serve as buffers against an invading enemy, were also deemed worth fortifying.

Not long after daybreak, the inhabitants of most towns and villages were well into their busy day. Some men went directly to the fields and did not return until sunset, while others, shopkeepers and craftsmen, busied themselves in the marketplace, opening their establishments for yet another routine day. The shops and stores there provided the goods and services that met the many needs of the community, furnishing items necessary for daily living. As one walked the narrow streets one would find children playing ball or other games, while their parents and neighbors concentrated on more important matters.

Though usually dirty, the marketplace was, nevertheless, the center of activity—alive with smells, sights, and sounds, all guaranteed to leave strong impressions. Here one could interact with residents in the community and sometimes with people from other lands.

Many of the outlying "Greek" cities held weekly "fairs" and special festival-day markets. These provided a place to purchase foreign goods from every part of the Roman empire, including slaves and outrageously expensive luxury items of every description.

Daily markets attracted people from many social strata, though the people of first-century Palestine could easily be divided into three distinct groups. First, there were the Arab nomads. These wandering shepherds of the desert maintained a freedom that allowed them to live where they chose, and for as long as they wished, without the rigors and responsibilities of life in the towns or villages. Next were the common people from the settlements, the majority of whom were farmers, shepherds and craftsmen; they are the people of this book. Lastly, there were those who lived a richer, more sophisticated life in the large urban centers. Among these were merchants, landowners, government officials, religious leaders, and of course, wealthy foreigners; but these people were exceptions. Most people of the city were common folk who resided in sections resembling in many ways the small villages from which they migrated. These sections retained characteristics of the villages: closely packed houses, the local market and water well, everyone's acquaintance with everyone else, and the local gossip. These served to make urban life familiar and bearable.

The lack of town planning allowed haphazard development, which produced a maze of narrow, winding streets and alleyways. Most streets remained unpaved and rough, especially in the smaller towns and villages. In the hot, dry summer, the dirt and dust were unbearable, and in the wet winter weather, the mud was inescapable. The streets were so narrow, they easily became clogged with people and animals. The small private dwellings of the poor were packed together so tightly along narrow streets on steep hillsides that the roof of one dwelling would be the front yard of another.

The wealthy lived on the fringes of these congested areas in suburbs of large, solid houses with extensive gardens. Some of the middle class also lived on this fringe, while others lived in the more congested part of the city, often in houses within walled enclosures. These homes had second-story rooms allowing an entirely different lifestyle.

The importance of an adequate community water supply often required aqueducts for conveying water from outlying springs. In addition, many private houses had cisterns for storing water at home, eliminating the need for daily trips to public wells.

Most villages and towns of Palestine were known for their hospitality and friendliness, as these qualities were valued highly by first-century Jews. Since few inns existed, most villages made provisions for travelers or guests, usually in the form of an upper room. If such accommodations could not be provided, a traveler would have no problem finding a gracious family with whom to stay the night.

The towns and cities were allowed a fair amount of self-government. The Roman authorities permitted this freedom of self-rule as long as the required tribute was paid, order maintained, and Roman law observed.

■

The village guest chamber was a room set aside by the people of the village for the needs of a visitor or traveler. A distinguishing characteristic of the people of Bible lands was their sincere friendship and hospitality. To provide for the needs of a guest was not only a duty, but a joy.

The guest chamber, often an "upper room," also served as a kind of community center where the men of the village would spend the day or evening in leisure and conversation. Often during a long, hot summer day a large shade tree served as a welcomed substitute for the hot room.

A hired servant maintained the guest chamber, while village families would provide for the needs of guests. Supplying the necessities of food and bedding fulfilled an obligation to their community.

The villagers would also provide for the guest's animals in the small stable area under the porch. In villages where no guest house was available, travelers, as a rule, would be with an inhabitant as an overnight guest. Inns or hostelries were rare.

Porters carried enormous loads on their backs through busy streets or alleyways that were too steep or narrow for pack animals with bulky loads.

Garbage and refuse lay strewed in the streets and narrow alleyways in most towns and cities. In first-century towns the lack of sanitation facilities encouraged dumping refuse and waste into the public streets outside one's door. Refuse not thrown into the street, or into refuse pits, was put outside the city gates. The stench, flies, and maggots from the rotting garbage were especially bad in the heat of summer. City dwellers simply accepted such filth as a fact of life.

At the local well the women gathered each morning and evening to collect fresh water for the daily needs of the family. The world of the first-century woman centered around her home, and her daily trips to the well were some of the few times she ventured out from the house. The well provided the social center of the village and a daily meeting place for the women.

Using a small, unbreakable leather bucket to draw the water from the deep well, a woman then poured the water into a clay water pot. She carried the heavy pot home on her head and poured its contents into a larger clay storage jar. Meeting the family's daily needs normally required many trips.

The streets abounded with beggars asking for alms. The sharing of what one had with the poor was considered a distinguishing mark of a righteous man.

The shops of the craftsmen would be found in their own quarter, gathered together for mutual benefit. Workshops were usually small, dark rooms that opened on the street or alleyway. A large, open doorway encouraged passers-by to pause and watch the skilled craftsman at work, as well as to examine the display of his products.

Street lighting, when it existed, would be found at the city gates or main street intersections. Torches or oil lamps enclosed in hanging lanterns at selected sites, provided a few hours of weak and restricted light.

Boys played ball in the street or the open area of a marketplace. Younger children played other games, often imitating happy family occasions such as weddings and festivals, or sad occasions such as funeral processions.

The noisy packs of dogs that roamed the streets were tolerated only because the dogs devoured the garbage and waste thrown in the streets. Despised by the people, the dogs were treated badly, often cruelly.

In the local neighborhood market, goods and food stuffs would be purchased to fill daily needs. People bought the necessities each day in the immediate neighborhood on a need basis, and only in a quantity that could be consumed immediately, as there were few facilities for storing perishable goods.

The fuel often used in the cooking stove or baking oven was flat cakes of dried animal dung. A basket load of fresh dung would be gathered from stables and fields, mixed with straw to be carried home, dried, and stored on the roof for future use.

Towns and villages were built as compactly as possible on high or rising ground, with the houses so tightly packed that a village or town would often appear as a fragment broken off a large city. This compactness helped provide security to the smaller communities, but with the crowding also came poverty, petty quarreling, and litigation.

In the marketplace the public life of
first-century Palestine took place.
The market, located in a street or
open area, was an unending
array of stalls and
displays, where
goods such as
wheat or barley
would be measured
out, and fish, bread
or olives could be
found in abundance.
One could also find Arab
spice-sellers with a variety
of spices separated in
small bags ready for
immediate sale.

All markets had much in common, no
matter what the size or location—they were
rich in sights, smells, and sounds. The shouts
of vendors trying to attract buyers, the endless
bargaining and disputes, the noises from nearby
workshops, and the bleating and braying of the
animals being sold or loaded, all added to the
babel. The sights and smells also varied sharply,
changing every few feet. All these strong
impressions were not quickly forgotten.

Every Friday, the day before the Sabbath,
was a big market day for the Jews. This was
the day to purchase special items needed to
celebrate the weekly holy day that would
begin at sunset.

The needle's eye was a small wooden door built into the massive gate. After the main door was closed and barred at sunset, the small "needle's eye" allowed limited access without endangering the security of the sleeping city.

The city gates were the only means of entering a walled town or city. City leaders therefore gave great thought to the gates' placement and construction. The thick wooden doors were secured by means of a great beam or iron bar. To prevent the enemy's setting the wooden doors afire, the outside was often covered with brass or iron plates. In order to overpower the gate, a sharp right turn had to be made once an enemy was inside the outer doors. This forced assaulting troops to expose their unprotected right side. When open, the gate was also the center of public life, the place to meet, as everyone had access to the high vaulted room within it.

The gatekeeper closed the city gates at sunset and opened them at sunrise each day. The safety of the city often depended upon this protection, so his was a position of great responsibility. Sometimes the local military garrison had the duty of opening and closing the gates.

The city wall was a massive stone structure with a broad, deep foundation, supporting a lofty height topped by a crenelated (indented) parapet.
These indentations and a walkway provided protection to defenders.
Square towers stood at critical spots along the wall. Interior stairways
provided access to the storage rooms and barracks in these towers. Bastions
differed from towers in that they simply extended out from the wall,
allowing access to the flanks of those attacking or trying to scale the wall.
The distance between bastions would never be more than two bow shots
apart. The gate, often the weakest spot in the wall, had additional towers
for defense and also for a guard house and quarters.

The citadel was a fortress within a fortress. Always
built on the highest spot within the city walls, this
stronghold usually consisted of a palace, barracks,
storehouse, and tower, all within its own walls. When
a city was under attack the citadel was often the
final place of refuge and resistance.

CHAPTER · THREE

INSIDE MUD AND STONES

In villages, towns, and cities throughout first-century Palestine, the day began with the bright morning sun lighting the uppermost hillside dwellings, while those homes in the valley remained in darkness. As the sun climbed into the eastern sky, illuminating more and more houses, the different sizes and shapes of the structures became apparent.

On the highest ridges of the cities and towns, which received the longest daily period of the sun's warmth, stood the homes of wealthy merchants and foreign officials—luxury stone villas with enclosed gardens. Nearby were the two-story houses, also of stone, belonging to the middle-class towns-people—shopkeepers, craftsmen, and small landowners. Farther down, clusters of tiny boxlike structures housed the poorer farmers, shepherds, and laborers.

Unlike the homes of the wealthy, most of these small, drab dwellings served merely as places for chores, crafts, shelter and meals, not as centers for comfort and enjoyment where daily living took place.

As the daylight increased, the clamor of morning activities began filling the narrow, dirty streets. The noises of people, animals, and tools combined in a cacophony of sound where only minutes earlier all was dark, empty, and silent.

Since the first century, little research effort has been given to the home life or the modest houses of those who lived most of their lives in poverty. Although the remains of many buildings have been unearthed in Palestine, these have been the larger, stronger homes of the wealthy. Little was written about the daily lives of the poor or middle classes in ancient writings, but many detailed descriptions of the great cities and their immense palaces and temples, with the lifestyle of the wealthy elite, are presently available.

One reason we know so little about the poorer classes of this period is that few of their houses have survived. Only a small number of well-preserved examples remain, but from these we derive some clues about these structures and the life of the average Jewish families who lived in them. This lack of surviving structures is understandable when one considers the perishable materials, such as mud bricks, used in the construction of most small domestic structures; the continuous building and rebuilding of such houses throughout the centuries; wind and rain erosion; and the recycling of building materials from one period to build new houses in a later era.

Fortunately, the few examples of housing from the first century which have survived, and the fact that some homes in the Middle East are built the same way they were 2000 years ago, provide a glimpse of what we would have seen had we roamed the streets of those ancient villages and towns. We soon learn that the spacious courtyards, porticoes and gardens we romantically associate with New Testament times belonged only to the rich and powerful and were rarely seen outside major cities.

The lives of the wealthy were filled with luxury and comfort. Their homes were well furnished and had, by first-century standards, the most modern of conveniences, such as hot running water, baths, and, in some cases, central heating. Servants and slaves made life easy for the owners of these luxury homes.

In contrast, for the family members in most poor and middle-class homes, life centered around preparing and eating the daily food. Mealtime, the "breaking of bread," was much more than just feeding oneself; this enjoyable time together with family and friends served as a continual bond that kept the family unit strong.

The constant food preparation, which was only part of her work, required endless hours of toil for the woman of the house. Shopping for available food, gardening, grinding flour, butchering were all preliminary to the actual cooking of the food. She needed a strong back and a willing heart to provide the constant care the family required. The rearing of children and the endless chores—sweeping the house, washing dishes, weaving, sewing, mending, and washing clothes—took more hours, even then, than were ever available.

The people of first-century Palestine lived on the few kinds of local products that were seasonal and available, although usually in plentiful supply. One of the few imported products one hoped to find in the neighborhood market was dried or fresh fish, depending on the distance to the nearest large body of water—the Sea of Galilee, the Jordan River, or the Mediterranean Sea.

Perhaps the most important food was bread. Baked almost daily, the cakes and loaves were made of the exceptionally fine quality grain of Palestine, some of the best wheat in the ancient world. Many of the poorer families could not afford this and were forced to bake with a cheaper, coarser barley flour. A few loaves of bread, a handful of olives, vegetables and some local wine made up the basic daily diet of the peasants.

The woman of Jesus' time was a much-respected member of the family. Her constant concern and care for her husband and children helped to maintain the all-important family unit—a unit which could deal with hard, even cruel times, while still retaining hope for the future. A woman's only venture outside the home normally would be her daily trips to the well or spring for water, frequent trips to the local market for food and other available supplies, or weekly hikes to the stream for washing the family clothes, if there was one nearby. On these outings she would meet with her friends and neighbors for friendly gossip and to exchange local news. As a good manager and teacher, the woman also made certain all family members completed their assigned household duties and responsibilities.

Most days were long and hard for every member of the family. In the evening they gathered for the main meal, and, at sunset, they closed the doors on the harsh, outside world. The inviting light and warmth from a clay lamp and the cookstove, the satisfaction of a good day's work, and the "breaking of bread" with family members would end all too early as sleeping mats of woven rushes were unrolled on the hard dirt floor. Each person would soon lie down, wrapped in a warm wool mantle, as the small oil lamp cast feeble shadows on the rough plaster walls. On into the night the lamp burned, bringing with its dancing light a sense of comfort and security to the whole family.

As the first warm rays of morning light again fell on the houses clustered on the hillsides, a new day would begin for those who made their home in first-century Palestine—the land where Jesus lived.

■

The "house of clay" was a squat mud-brick dwelling surrounding a two-level, earth-packed floor. The family lived on the larger, higher level while the lower area was used for storage and for the care and feeding of the domestic animals.

Usually set upon a foundation of stone, the walls were built of handmade, sun-dried bricks of mud stacked to the height of one story. When the walls reached the desired height, wood beams and branches were laid across to support a roof of beaten clay. The interior walls would be covered with a thick coat of waterproof lime plaster, while the exterior might receive only a token whitewash. Clay and chips of limestone would be packed together to make the floor as hard and dust-free as possible.

With only simple furnishings, the cramped, dark, and smoky single room served as both kitchen and bedroom; as soon as the evening meal was completed the family would clear a space for the mats or mattresses used for sleeping.

Houses made of mud needed constant upkeep and seldom survived more than one generation. Mud from the walls frequently washed into the narrow street, while the roof required constant repacking and leveling.

The simple "insula" was a cluster of unpretentious private houses crowded around small courtyards. The walls and floors were constructed from rough-hewn black basalt (volcanic rock), with mud and small pebbles employed to bind the stones together. Wall construction of this type is not strong enough to support an upper story, so only a light roof was made of mud and long branches over beams.

The one-room stone house was a firmly constructed structure built of rough-cut blocks of limestone laid on a solid stone foundation. The irregular joints between the stone blocks were filled with limestone chips and mortar, while the interior walls would be completely covered over with a thick waterproof white plaster, the full extent of any finish or decoration. The higher platform, or family living area, was built on a stone arch, which provided for a small animal shelter and stable area beneath. The floor of the platform consisted of crushed limestone, sand, and pebbles, packed solid over the stone arched base.

A parapet wall around the roof provided a safe haven for family activities, while a crudely erected shade booth in one corner of the roof offered relief from the hot summer sun.

The private homes of the wealthy reflected the tremendous impact of Greek and Roman architecture upon the look of Palestine. This large stone house was built around a spacious courtyard, with both the upper rooms and roof easily accessible by a corbelled (projecting stone or timber) stairway. Such exterior stairways allowed for maximum interior living space, while smaller guest rooms extended along each side of the court. Many conveniences accompanied this style of architecture, including water piped into the house from storage cisterns; and with water came baths and toilets. Most remarkable for the times was a system of central heating channeled through the hollow floor and wall construction of this type of domestic architecture.

The "upper room" was the major feature of this sturdy two-story stone house. Such a house was generally a town or city structure, and the cut-stone and sturdy arch construction ensured the strength to support a second level. This special addition doubled the living area and often served as a dining area or guest quarters. The high-ceilinged lower level, as those in most stone houses, had a raised platform that served as the family living area, and the lower and smaller front area served for quartering domestic animals. The large, arched rooms, plastered walls, tiled floors, porch, and lattice-windowed upper chamber all provided, by Eastern standards, spacious living accommodations for a middle-class family. The upper room in these private houses was often let out to others, so that major festivals could be celebrated by those who didn't have the necessary space or accommodations. For dining purposes the upper room provided enough space to serve a fairly large group in relative comfort.

This fascinating collection of common housewares *shows the variety of objects one would have found in a home of Palestine in Jesus' time.*

In a house of the wealthy, variations of these same items performed the same basic functions, with the only differences being in the quality of workmanship or materials used in their construction.

1) Large wooden bowl
2) Portable clay oven
3) Woven sieve
4) Storage vessel
5) Clay brazier
6) Leather bucket
7) Straw mat
8) Copper tray
9) Clay platter
10) Clay storage cupboard
11) Pitcher
12) Wood storage chest
13) Cloth storage bag
14) Storage basket

15) Goatskin bottle
16) Baskets
17) Plaited palm-frond basket
18) Flat basket
19) Grain hand-mill
20) Wooden bowl
21) Large pottery basin
22) Woven reed mat
23) Padded mattress
24) Large clay storage jar
25) Storage vessel
26) Grain storage bin
27) Vessel
28) Straw broom

29) Vessel for boiling water
30) Basket
31) Jug
32) Water vessel
33) Storage vessel
34) Cooking pot
35) Clay cooking stove
36) Wine flask
37) Bronze hand mirror
38) Metal pan
39) Fish plate
40) Megarian bowl
41) Clay strainer
42) Jug

43) Wooden spoon
44) Knife
45) Spatula
46) Egg spoon
47) Die (dice)
48) Oil vessel
49) Clay oil lamp
50) Dish
51) Bronze jug
52) Needle and thread
53) Spinning spindle
54) Unspun wool
55) Potsherd holding hot coals
56) Basalt dish and grinding stone

57) Basalt mortar and pestle
58) Clay strainer
59) Serving tray
60) Cup
61) Goblet
62) Kneading trough
63) Stone measuring mugs
64) Cooking pot
65) Beaker
66) Terra-cotta lantern
67) Cooking dish
68) Clay dish

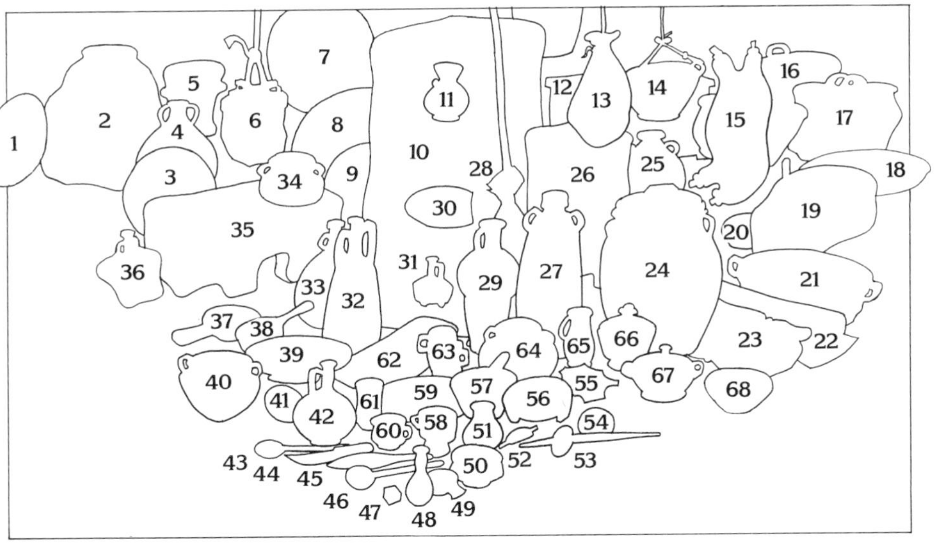

Spinning was done by the woman, who became so adept that she could spin while gossiping, walking, or even riding on a donkey; this task was usually done at home in odd spare minutes.

Food preparation was a main concern of every good wife and mother. Breakfast was usually eaten on the run: a handful of nuts, raisins and some bread or olives. Usually cheese, bread, olives, and possibly a handful or two of parched grain served them for lunch. The main meal, or evening meal, was often cooked stew, occasionally with meat and a side dish of vegetables, fruit and fresh bread. Preparation of this important meal required a great part of the woman's day, as most households did not have the facilities or cookware to prepare many dishes at one time.

The Nurturing of Children

A son remained in his mother's care until his fifth year. He then came under his father's guidance, to be instructed in a trade and to learn the laws and the duties of life. The daughter stayed under her mother's influence, learning domestic duties, until her marriage.

Minding the baby was made simple by a makeshift hammock. This type of cradle could be hung outside under a shade booth, or from the branches of a tree, as well as suspended from the wooden beams inside the house.

Dogs in Bible times were notorious scavengers and were treated with contempt by adults. Puppies were usually friendly enough to be kept by children as house pets, at least until the dogs grew larger and wilder.

Gathering twigs and branches was a task for the young girls or women of the household. The baking of the daily bread in the clay oven and the cooking of food on the stove often depended upon heat from this fuel.

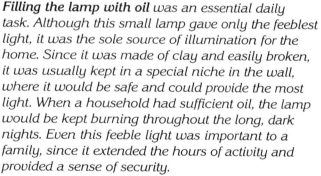

Filling the lamp with oil was an essential daily task. Although this small lamp gave only the feeblest light, it was the sole source of illumination for the home. Since it was made of clay and easily broken, it was usually kept in a special niche in the wall, where it would be safe and could provide the most light. When a household had sufficient oil, the lamp would be kept burning throughout the long, dark nights. Even this feeble light was important to a family, since it extended the hours of activity and provided a sense of security.

Heavy hauling was done by donkeys, or occasionally on the back of a man. Those who could afford it hired a porter. On the back of a porter, the goods could be moved more securely through the narrow, crowded streets.

Daily sweeping of the dirt floors would have been an appropriate task for a young daughter. The hard-packed mud and chip floor always needed a good cleaning.

The sifting of the grain was necessary to remove impurities. A sieve of woven mesh separated un-wanted seeds, chaff, weeds, and small stones from the grain before grinding in the mill. After the first milling, it was sifted again to eliminate bran, the skin or husk of the grain, before the final milling into a fine flour.

Sewing and mending of all kinds were constantly required of the woman. Most people had few changes of clothing, so the upkeep of their few garments was essential. Most clothes were of a simple cut, made at home and easy to care for. Embroidery decorated the plain tunic of a woman, and occasionally that of a little girl.

Fresh water from the local well or spring was needed at least twice daily, once in the early morning and again in the evening. At the well, as they drew their families' water, the women gossiped and exchanged news. Each carried her own leather bucket for drawing water. The women bore their large clay jugs on their heads.

Daily shopping for fresh fruits and vegetables was usually done at a neighborhood market. All the local products would be available, as well as a few imported products such as dried fruit, fish, and herbs. Because the methods for storage and preservation were extremely crude, both rich and poor had to shop daily.

Rolling the roof with a large stone roller after each rain was an important task for the man of the house. He rolled the surface to harden and flatten the soaked earth layer used in the roof construction, thereby preventing the water from penetrating. As one would suppose, grass and weeds of all kinds grew freely on an earth-packed roof.

Fresh goat's milk was valued highly. Along with its by-products of butter and cheese, milk made an important contribution to the family diet.

Washing clothes always took place at a nearby stream or pool. The woman first dipped the dirty garments in the water and rubbed them with a homemade vegetable alkali soap made from ashes. She then beat the garments individually and dashed and kneaded them on a flat rock. After rinsing and wringing, she spread the wet garments out to dry on surrounding rocks and bushes.

Daily Bread

In grain-rich Palestine, bread was indispensable. One kind of bread was a small, round loaf, and another was a thin, flat bread called "cakes."

Before using grain from the storage bin and grinding it to a fine flour on a hand-mill, they separated the grain from impurities with a sieve.

To make dough, a flour and water mixture was worked in a kneading trough with yeast and set aside to rise. The loaves were then put into a heated clay oven directly on the embers and watched with great care. The cakes, being very thin, could be baked on the outside of the oven, or on a small dish placed over heated coals.

The Graeco-Roman style of eating became the general practice of the more affluent throughout first-century Palestine. One lay on a mat or low couch while leaning on the left arm, thereby keeping the right hand free for eating. Normally the couches were arranged on three sides of a rectangular table, while the fourth side was left open for the service of the tables during the meal. Of the three couches, the one in the middle was regarded as the most honorable, and of the three places on it, that on the left held the guest of honor. The couch on the right was next to that in importance, the left couch being the lowest, with one spot occupied by the master of the house.

The host began the meal by serving the main-course meat, choosing the helpings for each according to his rank or honor. Using his fingers, each proceeded to eat. From a common bowl, sauces were scooped up, using hunks of bread. As prescribed by Jewish law, a benediction was pronounced at the beginning and at the close of each meal.

The basic foods of Palestine were few, but plentiful. Local agriculture usually provided enough, and in sufficient variety, to support the population with little dependence on imports. Because of the difficulty of preserving food in the warm climate, cooks prepared most foods as soon as possible after harvest; they prepared highly perishable foods, such as meats, for immediate consumption. Even bread, a principal food, became rough and dry to the palate after one day.

Only basic modes of cooking were possible, so only simple stews, porridge, and boiled vegetables could be prepared. Occasionally fish, roasted meats, game, or dried and caked fruits, along with seasonally fresh fruits and vegetables, accompanied those simple dishes. Wine, honey, and dairy products were available year-round.

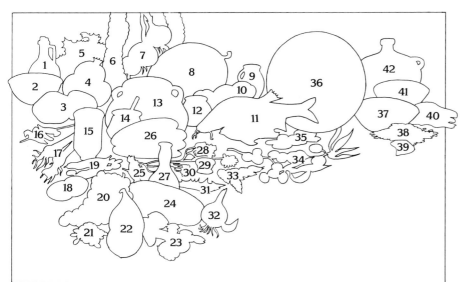

1) Vinegar (sour wine)
2) Butter
3) Cheese
4) Pomegranates
5) Lettuce
6) Dried figs
7) Onions
8) Melon
9) Leben (yogurt)
10) Apricots
11) Fish
12) Milk
13) Stew
14) Honey
15) Wine
16) Locusts (roasted or fried)
17) Leeks
18) Eggs
19) Beans
20) Grapes
21) Raisins
22) Figs
23) Nuts (walnuts, almonds, pistachios)
24) Cucumbers
25) Dill
26) Bread
27) Olive oil
28) Mustard
29) Salt
30) Cumin
31) Bitter herbs
32) Garlic
33) Mint
34) Olives
35) Dates
36) Fowl (roasted)
37) Sauce
38) Parched corn
39) Fig cakes
40) Thin bread
41) Porridge
42) Water

CHAPTER · FOUR

DRESS OF THE DAY

When we think of Bible times, our first thoughts are often images of the people and how they looked: an old man in a tattered mantle plowing a muddy field; a fisherman with his loins girded standing in a boat; a young woman in a long white tunic balancing a jar on her head; or children in dirty garments playing in the streets of a squalid hillside village.

Unfortunately, when we try to reconstruct the realities of Jesus' time, we find little information that can help determine, with any degree of accuracy, what everyday dress was really like. The Bible tells us little about clothing, for biblical descriptions are usually generalizations and the Greek words used are difficult to translate into modern terms we would know and relate to. Fabric is, of course, very perishable, so few examples of actual material, and no full garments of man or woman, have survived from that period. The other problem we encounter, when researching the dress of the period, is that the Jews were forbidden by their law to picture the human figure, so we have no contemporary art with clothing represented.

Enough clues are available, however, from ancient and biblical writings (such as the Talmud), from mosaics found in the remains of synagogues, from our knowledge of Graeco-Roman attire, and from the work of present-day archeologists, to let us establish the look of some basic garments worn in first-century Palestine.

The study of ancient Palestine has shown us that change always came slowly, and that there was little, if any, modification of these basic garments over the centuries. This was partly because of conservatism, as well as the strong traditions of the people, and also because peoples' needs and activities changed very little over the years. We should also bear in mind that strong foreign influences on this crossroad province were sometimes expressed in dress.

For example, the Graeco-Roman style of dress was totally accepted as everyday wear by many, especially the wealthy, and this gave a look to the period quite different from what we might expect. Basically, however, the common dress of the masses throughout Bible lands has always been simple and functional, and only the dress of the wealthy, the nobles, and the foreigner has varied from this rule.

A variety of basic garments existed, of course, as well as variations of fabric and weave, but the greatest difference was often in the kinds of decoration and color available. The selection of materials was not great, limited mainly to wool and linen, though some wealthy persons used such expensive fabrics as silk and cotton. Other materials available, but in limited use, were leather and the coarse, dark sackcloth.

The art of manufacturing cloth is very ancient, but at all times some materials were more esteemed, while others, such as cloth woven from the hair of animals, were considered of lesser value. Silk, the fabric of greatest price, and especially silk with precious-metal thread woven into it, was brought in by caravan. Some silk goods sold for their weight in gold. Linen was a versatile fabric that could be woven either in a delicate, transparent weave or into coarse, heavy cloth. The finer weave was always worn by those with position and wealth. As one of the most ancient materials, wool served as the principal cloth for everyday wear. So important was wool that the economy of the day depended greatly upon this resource. Cotton, unlike wool, was woven from the fiber of a plant and received limited used in Palestine during this period. Sackcloth was a coarse, dark, material made from the hair of animals. It was mainly used for tents, sacks, and the ritual cloth worn as a sign of mourning.

The greatest variety of weave came from commercial looms, but some cloth, especially wool and the coarser sackcloth, came from families who had small looms at home. The finer fabrics, purchased from the caravan traders, were usually dyed a variety of exotic colors, especially the popular deep reds and purples valued by the wealthy and powerful. The prevailing color of the cloth worn by the lower and middle classes was simply the natural color of the material, which could be brought to a brilliant white when bleached by the dry cleaner of the day, the fuller. Female garments always had decorations; most were highly decorated with embroidery or woven with different colored threads. A woman could easily and inexpensively give life and color to an otherwise dull garment by adding decorative designs made with needle and simple colored thread.

In many families there were members who could perform each of the tasks necessary to produce a complete garment. Beginning with raw wool, they would comb, wash, spin, weave, sew, and finally apply the appropriate decorations to their homemade garments. With style established and unchanging, size was the only factor necessary to determine in order to make a homemade garment.

There have always been general characteristics in the dress of those living in Palestine that, if studied even briefly, will tell us much about the clothing of the period. For example,

people generally disliked tight, close-fitting clothing, including undergarments. They also had strong feelings about body exposure of any kind, as well as an intense dislike for anything that firmly fixed clothing together, such as pins, knots, or buttons. These and other sentiments helped establish the basic garments that existed for many generations. Because they were both functional and comfortable, these and similar garments can still be seen in Palestine.

The dress of royalty and the privileged classes, as well as that of foreigners living in Palestine, was another matter. They, of course, dressed quite differently from the commoner in the street.

Other variations of clothing also existed, such as the dress of those with specialized occupations, particularly persons in large and important groups like the army or the religious establishment. Some of these styles developed through tradition, and some were adapted to the needs of the specialized functions of their wearers.

Another specialized attire, the dress of the desert nomad, has spawned great misunderstanding. The look of the Arab mounted on his camel, with his flowing robes and distinctive head covering, is often mistaken for that of the common dress of all Bible lands peoples.

To help develop an understanding of the dress of the men, women, and children in other lands and in other times, we should look more closely at how our own activities and environment affect our attitudes about our dress, what we wear, and when. We may find that some influences that affect how people dress today are similar to those influences that helped determine the dress of the people of Palestine in Jesus' time.

■

The short tunic, or "inner garment," was the indispensable garment of the masses. The tunic was usually made of coarsely woven wool or linen and often kept in its natural color. One type was this straight, shapeless bag that was woven in two pieces, front and back, then sewn together with holes for the head and arms. A tunic of this style was occasionally woven in one piece, without seams on the shoulders, making it a treasured garment. This billowing shape makes a belt (girdle) essential, especially when engaging in any kind of physical activity.

"Girding up the loins" was a means of tucking up the tunic to allow more freedom of movement, for the fit of garments could often hinder movement when the wearer engaged in work or some vigorous activity. To "gird" meant to pull up the tunic between the legs and tuck the end into the belt, thereby allowing for greater leg movements. Girding up the loins was also believed to provide extra strength to the body.

The full-length tunic was cut fairly straight and extended to the ankles. At the hem, slits on each side allowed for reasonable mobility as long as sudden or exaggerated movements were not required. This popular tunic could be worn with or without a belt around the waist, and was usually limited to indoors or familiar outdoor surroundings. Different styles in linen and wool were available, some dyed in a variety of colors.

The tunic of the wealthy man was a sleeved, full-length garment usually made of fine linen. On occasion a second tunic of wool or linen would be worn directly over this inner tunic.

The outermost tunic would often be dyed in a bright color or have thin stripes woven into the garment. Long sleeves, extending well beyond the fingertips, were split above the wrist allowing a separation so the hands could be uncovered. Although generally exposed, the hands could easily be concealed when in the presence of superior rank. Both tunics would be tied to the body by a richly decorated girdle belt.

The sackcloth tunic was a garment of great antiquity, worn as a sign of mourning or repentance. Woven from the coarse black hair of the goat, this stiff, rough garment would be worn against the smooth skin. A leather belt was wrapped around to hold this crudely fashioned garment to the body. While he wore this garment, a mourner would go without coverings on his head or feet.

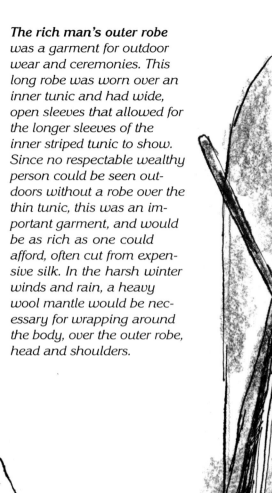

The rich man's outer robe was a garment for outdoor wear and ceremonies. This long robe was worn over an inner tunic and had wide, open sleeves that allowed for the longer sleeves of the inner striped tunic to show. Since no respectable wealthy person could be seen outdoors without a robe over the thin tunic, this was an important garment, and would be as rich as one could afford, often cut from expensive silk. In the harsh winter winds and rain, a heavy wool mantle would be necessary for wrapping around the body, over the outer robe, head and shoulders.

This mantle was the popular "outer garment" of the day, with great variety in size, weight, and quality. The heavier wool mantle would be worn on cold and wet winter days, and at night as a covering when sleeping. Jewish law forbade a creditor to keep this debtor's garment overnight. This simple square cloth was often drawn close to the body by use of a belt.

Blue tassels were sewn to the hem at the four corners as required by Jewish law. When the garment was wrapped around the body, two tassels hung in front, two in back, and they served as a reminder "to observe the commandments of God."

The mantle, or coat, was an outer garment worn over the thinner tunic. Much of the popularity of its shapeless style comes from the considerable freedom for movement it provided, as well as the decorative brown and black stripes that often ran from the shoulders to the hem.

The "upper mantle" was an outer garment worn by young and old alike, summer and winter. This mantle was similar to a square shawl, much smaller than the outer mantle, and worn as protection for the head and shoulders. Woven from wool of various weights, it was a convenient garment for seasonal protection against harsh elements—sun in summer, rain and cold wind in the winter.

Head Coverings

Covering for the head was important to all men; their hair and beards also received a great deal of attention and care. Most men kept their hair trimmed and clean and those who could afford it perfumed or anointed their hair for festive occasions. Boys and young men wore their hair short and thick, as a full head of hair was much esteemed.

A beard was considered the great ornamentation of the man, and he made a conscientious effort to keep it clean and in good order. Most beards were long, especially on older men, and constantly stroked by the proud owners.

The head covering most worn was the turban. Usually made of bleached linen, the white cloth was wrapped around the head several times, with a cap underneath. The cap could also be worn without the cloth wrap.

Another popular covering was a square cloth, held in place with a simple tie. In summer a cloth or leather tie was simply wound around the head and tied in the back to keep perspiration and hair off the face.

The belt, purse, and ring were popular accompaniments to the dress of the day. The girdle belt kept the billowing garments close to the body. The plainest kinds were made of folded cloth or leather strips, while the finer ones of linen or silk cloth were adorned with precious stones and metal ornaments. In its folds various articles could be easily carried, making the cloth belt a practical item of dress.

The purse was often a small leather bag that could be tucked into the bosom or belt. Since garments had no pockets, this bag was necessary for carrying coins and other small, precious items.

Most men did not indulge in extravagant dress, but all liked jewelry. Key and signet rings were popular and were worn on the right hand or suspended by a cord from the neck.

Footgear was of two types, leather shoes and sandals. Sandals of the same type were worn by both men and boys for rough, daily wear. The hard leather sandals were usually homemade, with hide straps and an innersole attached by nails to an outer wooden sole.

Shoes apparently were worn mostly by the upper class. Made of softer leather and without a hard sole, they were probably limited to indoor wear.

The woman's tunic was so similar to that of the man's that Jewish law expressly forbade the exchange of garments. The main distinction was that the woman's tunic was longer and more fitted to the body. The plainness of the garment was often enlivened with decorations, especially embroidery around the neck and on the breast. The quality of the woman's tunic varied from a rough, heavy, woven wool to a fine, lighter linen fabric. A belt of cloth, often striped or decorated in some way, was usually worn to hold the garment close to the body. No respectable woman would go far from home wearing her tunic alone; she virtually always wore an upper mantle over this basic garment.

The dress of the wealthy woman was somewhat different, the main difference being a second tunic of fine, richly decorated linen worn over the thin inner tunic. Both tunics were wrapped by an expensively decorated belt, often made of valuable materials such as silk, and studded with precious stones and metals.

Foreigners living in Palestine and members of the wealthier class dressed in the customary Graeco-Roman dress of the day, a tunic stole and the mantle known as a palla.

The "upper mantle" was a simple wrap for covering the head and upper body, and was in common use throughout Palestine. The diverse climate required a heavy wool wrap in the winter and one with a lighter woolen or linen weave for summer wear. This flexible wrap could be used to veil the face, as a shawl, or as a bag for carrying small items. When a belt was used the fullness of the mantle enabled one to carry a considerable bundle in the loose folds or the bosom.

Another type of outer garment was a straight-cut sleeveless mantle. This was much like a sack with holes for the head and arms, and was usually held to the body by the belt. The upper mantle was also worn with this garment to cover the head and upper body.

The veil *was an important item of dress for all women. In public, women always covered the head and face with a garment of some type. The only exceptions were young girls, maid servants, or those of the very low classes. We do not know how strictly the standard of covering was followed. We do know, however, that women sometimes exposed their faces, and they certainly did this in their home environment.*

Long hair was the pride *of a woman of Palestine. In Jesus' day it was popular to braid it and, for the wealthy, to adorn the head with precious stones and metals, interwoven in elaborate hairstyles. Many Jewish women of the upper class also adopted the Graeco-Roman hairstyles.*

Early Christian women were discouraged from wearing the elaborate foreign styles or even plaiting the hair, in favor of wearing it in a simple, straight manner.

Ornaments and Toilet Articles

Personal ornaments were many and varied, including a Roman "fibula" pin and highly prized earrings. Toilet articles might have included a perfume bottle, a wooden comb, eye-shadow stick, makeup palette, and a bronze hand-mirror.

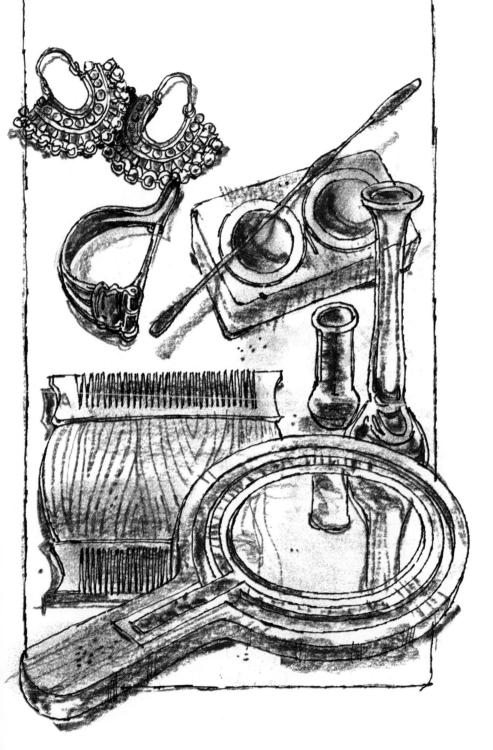

The innermost underclothing seems to have been of various shapes, but of specified cut. A loincloth or short skirt was one type, while the most popular was surely a long, light linen garment, straight and sleeveless. It is known that the male priest wore a different type of drawers, a style that may also have been worn by others, certainly men.

The heavy wool mantle was the principal outer garment worn most of the year. It provided the best protection against the harsh, often extreme environment. The heavy waterproof weave of the wool fiber protected the body against the cold, wet winter days and served as a warm covering at night while sleeping.

This common tunic was worn by both boys and girls, with the length being the major difference in the cuts. An everyday, all-purpose garment, it was made of woven wool for winter, and lighter linen for summer wear. Children's tunics were usually kept in their dull, natural color with a small amount of decoration often found on the girls' garments. To allow the necessary freedom required by active young people, they seldom wore a belt.

The covering for the head for children was not elaborate, but simple, protective, and like that of their parents. A woven cap, or simply a square cloth held in place with a cloth tie, provided a boy with the necessary protection from the hot summer sun or cold winter winds and rain. A large cloth placed over the head and wrapped around by an upper mantle usually provided the head covering required by a small girl or young woman.

Swaddling the Newborn

Immediately after birth, the infant was washed and then rubbed with salt to make the skin firm and tight. He was then wrapped in swaddling clothes which gave him a mummy-like appearance. A square cloth, folded over the child with bands tied around the tight little bundle, served to keep the body warm and straight. The wrap would be loosened occasionally and the infant rubbed with olive oil and dusted with powdered myrtle leaves. Swaddling would continue until the child was several months old.

CHAPTER · FIVE

THE FRUIT OF THE FIELDS

The pages of the Bible brim with references to the everyday life of the farmer in Palestine. As farming was the principal occupation of the people of the Bible, agricultural scenes and terms were commonplace and known to all. It was a noble work that had been handed down to the farmers of Jesus' time from the first plowman, Cain, son of Adam.

The farmer had always to live with a basic faith and hope that seed once buried would come alive and grow, a belief that the autumn rains would come and rouse abundant crops from the parched earth. Given to them by their God, this land fulfilled these hopes and rewarded their faith by providing for their needs. This truly was the land of promise.

Palestine included a variety of terrain and climate. In the north, the Galilee region was considered the garden spot of Palestine, the heart of the wheat belt. Its rich, red soil was dotted with groves of green fruit trees and covered with a patchwork of cultivated fields. Above these golden fields, nestled on the slopes of the broad green valleys, were many of Palestine's most prosperous villages and towns.

The southern part of Palestine was different, as steep mountains of barren deserts made up a great part of the Samarian and Judean landscape. The rocky, parched hills left little fertile soil with few agriculturally inviting areas. Figs, olives, and grapes were the products of this barren landscape. In the valleys, olive groves and vineyards and some grain fields would have been found; on the slopes, terraces of fruit trees and more vines. Almost all other areas were used for grazing animals. In Samaria and Judea, terracing effectively curbed erosion, but mainly the farmer benefited from

terracing because it provided more tillable soil for his vines and fruit trees. In this area, given predominantly to grape and olive production, there was a considerable number of fruit trees of other kinds. In the neighborhood of Jerusalem lay great vegetable gardens. In the semi-tropical Jordan Valley agriculture was limited and consisted mainly of figs and dates, so that, from an agricultural standpoint, the area possessed little significance.

Wheat was by far the most important crop and the main product of an agricultural cycle that began with the coming of the fall rains. Only after these rains had softened the hard parched earth could a farmer begin preparing the soil. He would plow the top layer of soil in one direction, sow the seed, then plow in another direction to bury the seed.

Harvest would commence only a few months later as reapers carefully cut the ripened grain by hand and hauled it to the threshing floor. Harvest was a joyous and extremely busy time for the whole village. On the threshing floor the grain was separated from the unwanted chaff, then cleaned and hauled away for safe storage.

Many other important field crops were growing during this cycle. Millet was grown mainly for animal fodder, but the farmers' only commercial crop was flax. A unique crop, flax was dried after harvest and processed into a thread used to weave the popular but expensive linen fabric.

In April and May a sweet, delicate aroma from the developing fruit permeated the entire countryside. While the major grain harvesting activities were underway, the vine was just coming alive. Only after the grain was harvested and stored could the farmer turn his complete attention to the vine. From the fruit of the vine of Palestine came a superior wine which was in demand everywhere, even to the outer extent of the empire. Judea had the perfect climate and terrain for the grape, and Judea claimed the grape "king," as attested by the many towns named for this agricultural activity.

To "tend the vine" required a devotion unlike any other agricultural venture. The process needed constant attention, for when the vine was neglected the quality and quantity of the grape quickly deteriorated. Producing a good wine necessitated proper and careful harvesting of the ripened grape, as well as crushing, pressing, and fermentation, before consumption of the long-awaited product was possible.

The fig was another common fruit. According to ancient legend, the fig tree is identified as the tree of knowledge. This adaptable and hardy tree will grow in almost any soil, and when cultivated properly it will produce an excellent fruit. Normally a tree will provide two crops annually, with the early fruit sparse but large, and eaten directly from the tree. The late fall crop of figs was the major crop, and was dried for winter consumption. In Jesus' time they would be dried in the sun and strung upon a cord, or mashed and made into cakes for easy storage even over long periods. Although the fig tree has always been highly valued for its fruit, it is also appreciated for its beauty and its deep, cool shade.

The olive was also an important crop that touched every aspect of daily life, from its use as the "meat and butter" of the peasant, to the many uses of its all-important oil. The wood of the olive tree provided a beautiful and highly esteemed, close-grained hardwood used for woodworking.

The olive tree was the "first of the trees" in Bible lands. Slow to mature, the olive required many years before bearing a significant crop. Once producing, it was capable of providing in abundance for hundreds of years.

Harvest celebrations would begin shortly after the precious crops of oil, grain, wine and fruit were in safe storage. Storage always posed a problem and required considerable planning and facilities if the people were to live off the fruits of the fields through the long, non-producing winter months.

The entire crop of most peasant farmers was required for their personal consumption. Only if one had an overly abundant harvest could the surplus be distributed and sold in markets at Jerusalem and other large towns. Wealthy farmers with large fields produced rich crops every year. Their special granaries and storerooms accommodated the great quantities harvested until the producers exported their commodities to other regions of the empire.

The "fruits of the field" from this rich and diverse land had always provided products that were in demand, not only in Palestine proper, but in foreign lands as well. Season after season Palestine's grain, wine, and olive oil were exported throughout the empire. The abundant harvests that provided in such excess proved this area to be truly blessed as a land "flowing with milk and honey."

The tenure of village lands was established by distributing fields for set periods, with certain conditions of possession. To keep the distribution fair to all, workable fields were parceled out by drawing lots from a pot. Each year the hopes and dreams of the village farmer depended upon this chance draw.

With great anticipation the villagers gathered annually to determine the land each would work for the coming season, as well as to resolve any problems that might arise over ownership rights. These rights were carefully protected during the farmer's tenure.

Plowing was a strenuous task that required a strong guiding hand and a steady eye to avoid stones and keep the furrow straight. Because the soil was dry and hard, the farmers waited for the autumn rains to soak and soften it before beginning their plowing.

The crude, wooden plow changed little over the centuries. An iron sheath covered the plowshare, which did little more than scratch the surface, never turning it over or breaking up the clods. The plow was drawn by oxen and was light enough to be carried to and from the field each day. Every farmer yearned to own his own plow and oxen team.

Sowing began when a suitable seedbed had been prepared by plowing.
The farmer usually scattered the seed by the broadcast technique—flinging
a handful at a time. This method effectively distributed seed over a broad
area. Never far behind, flocks of birds snatched up what had just been
scattered. Some of the sown seed fell on hard, stony soil or rocks and was
quickly burnt by the sun. To cover the seed for germination, and to protect
it from the birds, the farmer immediately replowed the newly sown field
in another direction.

The locust, *a flying insect that travels in swarms, devours every bit of vegetation in its path, including crops and fruit trees. Locusts were often eaten. Preparation usually included removing their wings and roasting them on a stick.*

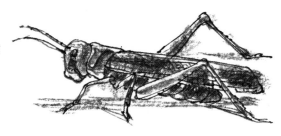

A large-wheeled cart, *laden with sheaves, was dragged creaking to the threshing floor. The driver moved the cart very slowly on his many trips to move the sheaves, in order to minimize loss of the dry ripe grain while en route.*

Gleaners were allowed to follow the binder and collect any of the precious grain not cut and bound. Gleaning could provide the poor with enough grain to make their bread throughout the winter months. The Bible commands the farmer to leave the corners of his fields for poor neighbors to glean.

The harvest of the wheat was usually done by the farmer and his family, including women and children. Only occasionally did he hire extra reapers.

The reaper grasped a handful of ripened stalks and, with an iron-bladed sickle in his other hand, sheared off the stalks with such care that scarcely a grain fell. The stalks were then carefully laid down for gathering and binding.

The binder followed the reaper, gathering up the stalks to bind them into a sheaf. The sheaves were set aside for collection as the binder moved on to gather up his next sheaf.

Donkeys were also used to carry the sheaves from the fields to the threshing floor. They were often so heavily laden that only their hooves and nose protruded from under the burden.

On the threshing floor the farmer separated the grain from the chaff. The sheaves were broken (untied) and the stalks spread out so that the threshing sled could work most effectively. Because winnowing followed this preliminary separation, the hard threshing floor had to be on a high, windy spot.

The threshing sled was an implement used for freeing the grain from the stalk and chaff as it lay upon the threshing floor. Sharp basalt rocks and flintstones, embedded in the underside of the heavy wooden sled, helped break the grain from the hull. The combination of man, beast and sled provided fast, effective threshing.

Winnowing *was the method used for cleaning the newly threshed sheaves. When the mix was tossed into the air, the heavy ears of grain would fall in a pile on the threshing floor and the unwanted chaff was carried away by a light breeze.*

To prevent the theft of his precious, winnowed grain, a farmer might sleep beside it on the threshing floor until it could be moved to a secure storage area.

Flailing was another method of threshing. The flail consisted of two long wooden sticks, tied or hinged together, and was swung overhead by the thresher to beat out the grain. When only a small quantity of sheaves needed threshing, the flailing could take place in a large limestone wine press. This vat contained the precious crop so effectively that not one grain would be lost.

The grain was carried to storage in baskets as soon as it had been cleaned. Transporting the grain safely to the storage room or silo required great care and many trips.

Sifting separated and removed small foreign matter from the winnowed grain. The sieve was rhythmically shaken until all the grain fell through the mesh and only the chaff, stones and grit, or other impurities remained. This residue was then thrown off. Women or young girls carried out the sifting process, often repeating it many times.

Constant care was required to maintain a vineyard, for a neglected vine quickly degenerated. As the heat of summer intensified, the vine required more and more attention to keep it producing an abundant crop. Pruning, done in the early spring while the branches were barren, removed unproductive sections which would leech nutrients from healthy branches. It was also important to keep the soil around the vine loose and free from thorns and weeds.

The vineyard and its vines *were highly prized possessions. An owner gave considerable attention to protecting the valuable plants and their crop. A farmer usually trained his vines to trail along the ground, and installed props to keep the large clusters of fruit off the ground. Some vines were pruned and trained to grow over a large prop, or on a trellis, or over terrace walls.*

The vineyard was usually located on a stony hillside enclosed within its own protective wall, with a high watchtower and a wine press situated in one corner.

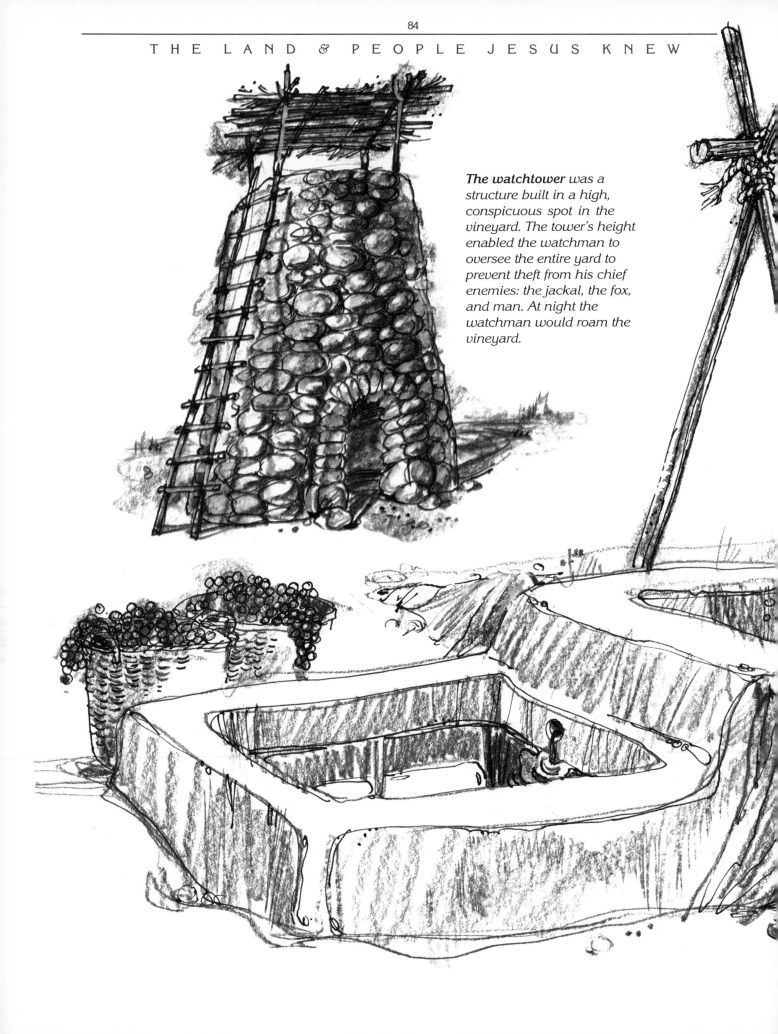

The watchtower *was a structure built in a high, conspicuous spot in the vineyard. The tower's height enabled the watchman to oversee the entire yard to prevent theft from his chief enemies: the jackal, the fox, and man. At night the watchman would roam the vineyard.*

The wine press was carved out of the soft limestone in the vineyard hillside. The press featured two basins, the upper being the largest, approximately one foot deep, with a drain to the lower basin. The smaller collecting basin was carved much deeper to hold the juice that flowed from the pressing basin.

The grapes were gathered and carried to the press in baskets. The barefooted treaders began stamping the juice from the grapes, maintaining rhythm by singing and clapping. This was a joyous time for everyone. A wooden crossbeam with straps helped the treaders keep their balance. After the treading was completed, the remaining grape skins were scraped to the center of the basin and pressed with weights to extract the last ounce of juice.

The juice collected in the lower basin was drawn off and left to settle in large jars. During that time fermentation took place, and the impurities settled to the bottom. The new wine was then transferred to other jars or skin bottles for storage.

THE FRUIT OF THE FIELDS

The fig, an important sweet fruit that ranked high as a source of food, was eaten both fresh and as a dried winter staple. The large fig tree, with wide spreading branches, produced two crops annually. The early figs were prized for their delicate flavor and were eaten fresh from the tree; the late figs were the main crop and were dried for use in the winter months. The harvest was a joyous time. Every family covered its roof with large quantities of figs drying in the sun.

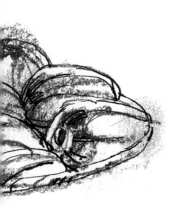

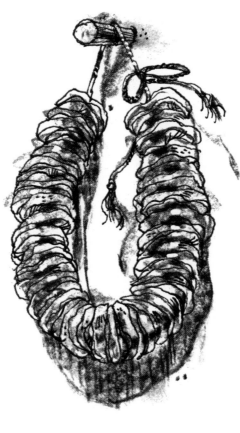

The dried fig provided important nutrition during the winter months. The sun-dried, shriveled fruit could be mashed and made into "cakes of figs" and stored in bins, or kept whole and strung upon cords for hanging in storage rooms.

The olive harvest was the last ingathering of the agricultural year. All olive groves were harvested by their owners on a fixed day so that no one would be free to collect olives from his neighbors' trees. Fruit remaining after that day could be gathered by anyone.

Harvesters first shook the olive trees, then beat them with long sticks, and finally picked them clean from ladders. This harsh method was hard on the trees, and often stunted the following year's crop.

The olive mill was a large, round basin carved out of solid limestone, with a large rolling stone attached to a pivot post by a long axle. The mill was built for the sole purpose of crushing the oily pulp of the olive.

The fruit was carried from the trees and spread out in the circular trough of the rolling stone. The crushing surface was recessed, and the stone wheel ran upon a raised rim. This allowed only the fruit and not the seed to be crushed, since a mashed seed would give the oil a bitter taste and smell.

The operator pushed the axle around the mill, and as the wheel rolled, it crushed the fruit in a few turns. The oily pulp was then removed from the trough and placed into woven fiber bags for the next step in the process—pressing the pulp in an olive press.

Milling *small quantities of olives was often accomplished on a hard surface by using a stone or house-roof roller. With care the millers could crush the meat of the fruit to a pulp without crushing the seeds. The pulp was then gathered up and placed into the woven pressing bags.*

The pressing bags were also used to press small quantities of olive pulp under the stamping feet of women and young girls. The extracted oil would be channeled into small collecting jars; the filled jars were poured into larger standing jars in which the fresh oil stayed until the impurities settled and the pure oil could be drawn off and stored.

The olive press was an ingenious device used to press the oil from the olive pulp. After harvesting, the ripe olives were crushed in the olive mill and then collected in woven fiber bags. The bags were stacked in the press and placed under pressure to squeeze out the valuable oil.

The indoor screw-press illustrated was particularly effective because of the tremendous pressure that could be applied to the fruit pulp. Other types of olive presses used a beam with weights attached to apply the pressure. The pressure was applied for several days, during which the collecting vat or jar was continually being filled.

Although only a trickle of oil would come at the beginning, it increased gradually until a steady flow poured into the collecting vat or jar. There it remained until the pure oil came to the top and the dross and water sank to the bottom. The oil was then dipped out and poured into storage jars.

Storage *was the final step in the agricultural process. It was also one of the most important, for only proper storage would preserve food for the nonproductive winter months.*

Grain was stored in bins, silos and large clay jars. Oil and wine were typically kept in smaller jars, but some wine was stored in new, flexible skin bottles. Dried figs could be mashed into cakes or hung whole on cords. Vegetables and fruit were often kept in dark, cool storage rooms.

The Grain Silo

An underground silo was used mainly for the storage of grain. Though usually cut into solid limestone, occasionally some were sunk into the soil and lined with stone. A grain silo always received a final protective coat of thick, waterpoof plaster.

This cross section of a silo shows its basic construction, shape, and the broad opening which was concealed with wood, soil, or stone for security reasons. Grain could be preserved for many years in a dry, well-constructed and sealed underground silo.

CHAPTER · SIX

A LAND OF SHEPHERDS

The New Testament abounds with the symbols of the "good shepherd" and his flock. Ancient records show that long before the Israelites became settled farmers, they were a pastoral people with huge flocks of sheep and goats. Many of the great men of Bible history, such as David and Moses, were described as men who care for a flock: shepherds. At the time of Jesus, shepherding was still an important occupation and virtually unchanged since the early days of pasturing animals.

There were two distinct types of shepherds that we should know about in first-century Palestine. First, one whom we are all familiar with, was the nomadic tent-dweller who roamed the desolate desert fringes with his flocks. For this nomadic shepherd, sheep and goats were a major source of subsistence and the center of his lifestyle. The second, and the one we will deal with in this chapter, was the peasant shepherd. This shepherd lived in and was an integral part of a close-knit community. His shepherding varied in importance depending upon his location and individual needs.

Unlike the nomad, the peasant shepherd belonged to a village as a permanent resident, and this status gave him certain privileges. He possessed the right, for example, to feed his flock in the gleaned fields surrounding the village and graze them on the spring grass in neighboring hills. Only after this local food source was consumed did he move his flock to other areas. He first moved to the cooler mountain pastures in the heat of summer, and then, when fall and winter approached, moved toward the lower, warmer coastal plains and valleys.

The life of the shepherd was not easy, for he had to spend the greater part of the year out of doors in all kinds of weather, day and night. To keep warm in cold and wet weather, he wore a head covering and a heavy, water-resistant mantle. The mantle was especially helpful for sleeping out in the open countryside.

A rod, staff, and sling afforded protection for himself and his animals against predators and thieves. A shoulder bag carried his supplies and the only other item desired by most shepherds was a simple musical instrument, often a flute, to provide many pleasant hours of entertainment.

A good shepherd was an extraordinary person, and his concern and care for his charges was legendary. He lived an extremely demanding and arduous life, and often endangered himself to protect his flock. His concern for the well-being of his charges meant a constant search for good, safe pasture and sufficient water. At the watering places he often experienced unpleasant encounters with other shepherds. Rights for access to the precious water and the task of watering at wells with other flocks caused frequent bitterness and strife.

His flock usually consisted of both domestic sheep and goats. The broad-tailed Syrian sheep was a helpless and fearful animal which, without someone to constantly guard over it, was at the complete mercy of its enemies. Under the long, carmel-colored fleece was a meek, gentle, obedient animal which produced wool for clothing, and, of course, meat for the festive table.

The goats of Palestine were also of a Syrian strain. They were more adventurous than sheep and loved a good climb. While the sheep preferred to graze in the flat meadows, the goats clambered about the rocky hillsides. They were much more independent than sheep, and therefore harder to handle.

The shepherd taught both the goats and sheep to obey and respond quickly to his call. He constantly struggled to keep them out of the unfenced fields of ripe grain, or the dangerous cracks and crevices which temptingly lay all around. The shepherd made occasional use of dogs to help guard and handle the flock. The flocks were totally dependent on the guidance and protection of the shepherd and his dogs.

Some men, hopeful of having a flock of their own one day, would hire out to herd the animals of others. Most villagers had a few sheep or goats and would engage these hired shepherds to include their few animals in his flock. The "hireling" would take this flock out to pasture and return it each day. This was not always best for the animals, as hired shepherds were not apt to show the care and concern for the flock that the owner would.

Most shepherds cared only for their own animals, and in the evening brought their flocks to their sheepfolds for protection. The folds varied greatly in structure and size; some were round and some were square. In the open country, most were a high stone wall enclosure with a shelter. In the wilderness, a partial enclosure would often suffice or, better

still, a small cave in the hillside with an additional rough wall of stone was enough to protect the flock from thieves and preying wild animals. When away from the village fold, the animals were more restless and needed constant reassurance that they had the protection of the shepherd. For this purpose, and for mutual protection, many flocks were often brought together at the end of the day and enclosed in the same makeshift fold.

Shearing was hard and dirty work, done twice a year at the sheepfold by the shepherd and his helpers. They performed the first shearing at the end of summer grazing, and the second near the end of winter. The sheep were always washed before any shearing was begun and the fleece was washed again in the creek or pool immediately after the shearing. With most of the dirt and natural oil washed out, women would comb it, which took out more of the matting, then spin it into thread, and later weave it into cloth. If the fleece was to be exported, it would be packed into fabric-wrapped bales before being taken to a marketplace.

A shepherd possessed a deep love and concern for his charges, and in return received the complete trust of the animals of his flock whose needs he provided. His strong and noble character should impress us today, as it obviously impressed those of Jesus' time. ■

The shepherd of the New Testament symbolized God's care for his
chosen people, and man's ideal of human character. In the vast and lonely
countryside his life was not easy or comfortable, for he was dedicated to
fulfilling the needs of his flock. With strength, courage, and leadership, he
daily fed and watered his flock, and provided the safety it required.

The shepherd came to know his sheep by their individual characteristics. He delighted in knowing them well enough to give each a name, often based on an incident or a special trait of the animal.

They knew his voice and would follow only the call of their own shepherd. Each shepherd made a very personalized sound, unlike that of any of his fellow shepherds.

The shepherd's love and care extended to each animal under his charge, including this newborn lamb too feeble to follow its mother.

A shepherd often played for his flock on a musical instrument. The ancient, double flute was made of reeds bound together by cord. From only a few simple notes, the piper produced strangely appealing and haunting tunes.

At watering time, the shepherd drew cool water from a well and poured it into troughs from which the animals drank. In the heat of summer many of the pools and streams dried up, and the only water available was from deep wells.

Gear and Garb

The shepherd outfitted himself with simple, effective clothing and equipment. In cold, wet weather his dress consisted of a head cover, a girded woolen tunic, and a warm, woolen, waterproof outer garment which also served as a blanket for sleeping on the cold ground. Sturdy leather sandals protected his feet from thorns and stones.

His gear included a staff, a straight or crooked stick about six feet long, useful for climbing and handling the animals; a "scrip," or leather bag, used to carry everyday supplies such as food and utensils, as well as a few "lucky" stones for slinging; a woven leather sling with a web pocket; a small, collapsible leather bucket for drawing water from a well; and a light, unbreakable vessel which hung from his belt and contained drinking water.

When leading his flock to pasture, *the shepherd called his own out of the sheepfold, and when they had gathered about him he walked before the flock, always leading, never driving the helpless animals, as he anticipated their every need. This picturesque and prominent figure of Palestine led with strength, as the paths were often narrow, precipitous, and treacherous. The paths among the grain fields, between the tempting, unfenced ripe grain, were very narrow. Because his animals were forbidden to eat in fields of growing crops, the shepherd demanded complete obedience from his charges.*

If the flock of sheep and goats was exceptionally large, the shepherd would go before them while a helper or dog would follow behind. This rear guard gathered any stragglers and protected the animals from a possible rear attack by wild animals.

Watching over the flock at night *was the duty of the sheepfold doorkeeper and possibly his dog. Often, the task required more than one shepherd or hired watchman to provide the complete and constant protection required by the flock, especially at night. A shelter for the doorkeeper always stood on a high spot near the entrance to the fold.*

The sheepfold was an enclosure for the protection of the flock. After sunset or in harsh weather, flocks would be kept in large, permanent folds, under the watchful eye of the shepherd or doorkeeper. A low, flat stone structure was often provided to shelter the flock. Thorn branches covered the top of the stone wall to discourage predators or thieves. Away from the home sheepfold, a less-permanent enclosure would usually be built at an existing semi-enclosed area or cave.

The shepherd always counted his animals at the sheepfold door. As the animals entered or left the fold, they "passed under the rod" and were counted. When tithing the flock, the shepherd dipped the rod in a marking dye and brought it down to mark the back of every tenth animal.

Protecting the Flock

To defend his animals, the shepherd had only his wits and a few primitive weapons: the rod, sling, and crude knife.

The rod was basically a heavy club, two to three feet long, made from the larger, bulbous end of a tree root. Often studded with iron nails or sharp flint, it was a formidable weapon when swung or thrown.

The sling was a long-range weapon that could hurl a stone great distances with deadly speed and accuracy. Made of leather strips and pouch, it was an extremely effective weapon.

From the Flock

The sheep and goats provided many valuable, everyday products. The most important was wool, a sturdy fiber that was woven into fabric for clothing. Coats and caps were made from the skins, with the fleece turned in next to the body. The coarse hair of the goat was also woven into cloth, mainly for tent material, or for the heavy sackcloth outer garments. The skins of the sheep and goat were tanned and used as bottles for holding liquids.

There were other uses also. For a feast, a lamb or kid would be roasted. The rich milk of the goat would be used fresh or made into cheese. The horn of the ram was often used as a sounding trumpet—the *Shofar*.

Washing the newly sheared fleece was a women's task, done at a local stream or pool. Even though the sheep were washed before being shorn, the fleece required several washings with lye soap to remove the dirt and natural oil in the fibers.

Women beat out the excess water from the tangled, soggy fleece before laying it out on nearby rocks to dry in the sun.

Shearing relieved the animals of their valuable growth of fleece or hair. It was a festive time, for at long last the devotion and concern of the shepherd would pay off. The winter shearing took place in May, and a second shearing later in the year. Wool shorn at the end of summer, the second shearing, was considered to be of a better quality, as it was cleaner and less matted. The cleanest, and whitest had the most value.

The sheep market *was a major trading center and would be found near a main city gate. Because of the vast amounts of wool required by the textile industry, the animal that produced this basic raw material was an important asset. Throughout the years wool remained a keystone in the general economy of Palestine, the major product of the village shepherd and the pastoral nomad alike.*

In addition, at Jerusalem, worshipers at the temple required great numbers of sheep for daily sacrifice. Therefore, the Jerusalem market demanded animals for both secular and sacrificial purposes. Even in the temple area itself there was a flourishing trade in animals for sacrifice, sheep being a principal animal.

CHAPTER · SEVEN

WOOD, CLAY, AND WATER

As the morning sun broke over the surrounding hills of first-century Palestine, the working people in the small one-room houses of the town and villages began the usual long, hard routine of their day. Quickly they awoke, then washed and dressed for the labor that awaited them. After a breakfast of often no more than a handful of parched grain, a piece of bread, a cup of water, and maybe leftovers from the evening meal, they set off to their labor in the fields and vineyards, or, if they were craftsmen, in their workshops.

At about the same time, some workers, the fishermen, were just arriving home after a long, hard night of labor on the Sea of Galilee. In first-century Palestine fishing was considered an honorable occupation, even though fishermen, in general, were a tough lot. Maybe it was the strenuous work, exposure to the elements, and the long nights of toil that left them crude in manner and rough in speech. They formed a distinct class and often lived with other fishing families in a community close to the water. A good fisherman was known for his ability to bear long hours of toil without success and still be ready to try one more time to make that "big catch." Some of the first Christians came from this hard-working group.

The Sea of Galilee was the center of the fishing industry in Palestine, for its waters abounded in freshwater fish. The sea was usually crowded with fishing boats of all kinds and sizes. So rich was the bounty that these boats often harvested fish from shoals so vast that they churned up acres of surface. For most of the inhabitants along Galilee's shores, fishing was the main livelihood.

The early mornings were the busiest time as boats returning from a night of fishing were made secure, nets were set out to dry and, most importantly, the fish were sorted into baskets for delivery to the nearby markets. Some of the catch would go to a fishery for processing. At a fishery the fish would be pickled, smoked, or sun-dried for discriminating markets as far away as Rome.

Those who spent their lives in the many fishing towns on the shore lived from and for fishing. Even without a boat they could fish the rich shallow waters with the small, effective casting net, or simply with a hook and line.

The commercial fisherman's two main implements were, of course, his boat and his nets. He lovingly cared for both, even though the care monopolized almost every hour not spent fishing.

As the morning sun rose higher and the night fisherman took his rest, other workers opened their workshops and prepared for the day's labor. The carpenter could be found amidst the clean smell of freshly cut wood in a small shop, the dirt floor covered with shavings and sawdust. On any given day his work could include constructing or repairing a plow or threshing sled, cutting a roofing beam, or shaping a yoke for a new team of oxen. He also supplied the constant demands for new doors and door frames, or a storage chest, as well as repairs of all kinds. Occasionally he would assist on larger building projects, such as the construction of a wood balcony, doors, or stairs for a new synagogue. Sometimes a master carpenter would be commissioned to build a holy object such as a Torah cabinet, used for storing Scripture scrolls.

The carpenter was a proud worker, practicing a trade that required highly developed skills in all aspects of wood working, from cutting rough lumber planks and beams to the finishing of highly polished personal items.

The wood which the carpenter used varied depending upon the job requirements: cypress, oak, ash, sycamore and olive were most readily available. For special projects he sometimes imported expensive cedar, or for small items used the stock of the vine. With a few basic tools and his considerable skill he could produce intricate dovetailed, mitered, and dowelled joints. His final products were often marvels of skill and patience.

The work of the potter also held an important place in the lives of those in Jesus' time, for the products of his wheel served a wide range of the basic needs of his neighbors. The potter's clay products provided toys for the children, lamps for light, and clay pots for cooking and storing foodstuffs. Even the broken pieces of a pot filled many needs; potsherds became scoops, game markers, bottle covers, dishes, or a surface upon which to write receipts.

Even though his craft was considered dirty and messy, the potter performed a great service to the community and must have been proud of his fine work. To mold, with his own hands, globs of ugly clay into beautiful, practical vessels must have helped offset his small compensation.

Because some styles of pottery had a long life, and because fired clay endures indefinitely, many pieces have survived until today, providing the archeologist with an effective system for dating events in ancient Palestine. Recovered pottery teaches us a great deal about the people and their lifestyle.

Pottery production was an unattractive occupation. The dirty work area and the intense black smoke from the kiln projected a negative image, and over the years forced the potter to work outside the city walls. He worked and gathered his clay in an area often called the "potter's field."

At the center of his shop the potter sat at his wheel. The invention of this fast-spinning wheel, centuries earlier, revolutionized the pottery industry, since forming pots on a wheel vastly improved their structure and design, as well as greatly increasing production. In fact, since the fast-wheel the production of pottery had become one of the major manufacturing industries of Palestine. In addition, just before this period, techniques for molding vessels and lamps had been developed that enhanced quality consistency and increased production speed. Other areas of the shop were used for preparation of the clay and for storage of completed, but yet unfired, vessels. Another important facility was the blackened kiln which stood in the yard not far from the shop. A small area was always set aside to display the vessels created in the shop.

As tradition dictated, these noble workers, the fisherman, carpenter and potter, used simple elements such as wood, clay, and fish gathered from the waters to provide for the basic daily needs of those who lived in Palestine. The men of this prominent group of workers received the respect of the people in their communities, not only for their skills, but also for their dedication, hard work, and honesty.

Renowned for their character, these men were held up as examples, illustrating important points in biblical messages. The common and familiar aspects of daily life were often used to illustrate the thoughts and ideas of both Judaism and Christianity.

In his humble workshop, among the chips, shavings, and sawdust, the carpenter shaped the wood items required by his neighbors. In addition to making standard items such as plows, yokes, or small tables, he contracted to design and build custom items as well. He also did construction work, since every building required a wood door and frame, as well as a variety of other wood items.

The bow-lathe was a crude primitive tool; yet, in the hands of a skilled craftsman, it produced decorative spindles and bowls that were a marvel of talent and workmanship.

The wood was turned by a leather strap pulled back and forth by a bow. This motion drove the lathe and allowed the cut to be made in the turning wood.

A variation of this bow-lathe was also used for turning vessels (cups, bowls, and platters) of soft limestone.

Sawing trees into boards was part of the carpenter's work. He had to fill his own need for wood to complete his projects. He would also provide the beams used in the ceilings of buildings.

With a large bronze saw, and with the aid of other workers, the carpenter would cut thin boards from a tree trunk. The boards were usually shorter than the cut illustrated here, as most trees in Palestine didn't get a chance to become large, nor did they grow straight.

From the Tool Box

The carpenter tools displayed represent most of those required in the woodworking trade. The select few illustrated are mentioned in ancient sources and give us a good idea of the tools that were indispensable.

The bow drill was one of these tools. It was held in one hand by the handle and rapidly set in motion by drawing the attached bow back and forth. The other tools displayed are the saw, mallet, adze, plummet and line, chisel, rule stick, plane and squares. The compass, iron nails, knife, and marking tool would have been handy, but optional.

The carpenter below is proudly showing a newly completed yoke, demonstrating the quality work produced with these simple tools.

For the potters of Palestine the main object was to produce practical vessels designed to fill daily needs. Yet they produced many items that possessed beauty as well as utility.

The potter was proud of his work and skill with the unpredictable material. He could create from the ugly clay everything from an infant's rattle to a storage bin, and all the different types of pots, jars, dishes, drain tiles, and oil lamps required by those working and living in this harsh land.

The range of products was great and varied, and only a few of the many are represented below.

Light for Everyone

For thousands of years oil lamps were made on the potter's wheel as other clay vessels were. Shortly before the Roman period, however, decorated mold-made lamps made their appearance, revolutionizing clay lamp production.

Lamps made on the wheel were difficult to produce, while mold-made lamps were stamped out quickly and simply. Negative casting molds were made of stone, plaster or baked clay, the lamp top coming from one mold and the bottom from another. When the top and bottom castings were "leather hard," they were pressed together and the joint was smoothed over, sealing the two parts together.

Special workshops existed solely to produce mold-made clay lamps, both for export and for domestic use.

The potter kneaded his clay by treading and by clapping globs of clay together as one of the first steps in the process of creating a product. This treading was done in a rhythmic fashion, forming patterns in the clay with his feet to make certain all parts were kneaded equally.

The clay was often used just as it was found in nearby beds (except for the removal of stones and foreign matter), and it could be used for large, heavy vessels or bins. For finer burnished ware the clay was allowed to stand in settling basins, and the fine watery upper layer was skimmed off. After the excess water had evaporated, the remaining damp clay was excellent for throwing small, fine vessels with thin walls. The potter always sought out colored clays that would add pigment to the normal tan clay. He usually added a tempering ingredient to the clay mixture to improve its workability as well as reduce shrinkage and cracking when fired.

Drying, Finishing, and Firing

After a vessel came off the wheel it was carefully air-dried before the pottery was fired in a kiln. For proper drying the finished pieces were set in the shade until leather hard; such slow drying prevented cracking as shrinking occurred.

Updraft clay or stone kilns of two levels were usually used to fire the pottery. The lower level contained the fire-pit fueled by wood, dung cakes, thorn or grass. The temperature in the upper chamber was slowly increased to a range of 700°–900° C. so as not to crack the vessels. The fuel produced a smoky fire which drew the oxygen out of the clay and baked the clay harder at a lower temperature than was possible with a clean-burning fuel. As the firing could take up to three days, this provided considerable savings in fuel.

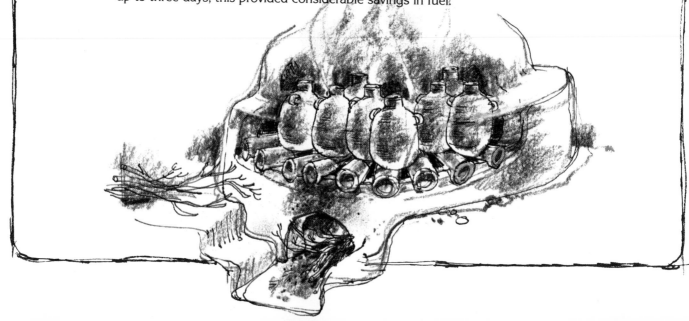

The potter began the counter-clockwise rotation of the wheel with a kick to the lower disc. He then threw a plug of kneaded clay upon the wheel and forced it to the true center of the rotating wheel. With a large dish of water and some extra clay at his side, the potter was ready to shape a vessel.

   With his hands, the potter drew the rotating clay up to form sidewalls until the desired height, shape, and wall thickness were obtained. After completion, the lower attachment was cut off and the base was often indented so it would stand on a rough surface. Handles or spouts and decorative elements were added before the vessels were fired in the kiln.

The casting net was thrown with a broad spinning motion over shallow water. The net fell in a ring as the weights on the perimeter of the fine mesh dragged it down, and as the net sank it took the shape of a dome which enclosed the fish. The fisherman drew it closed with a line attached to the center and collected the catch entangled in the mesh.

In the late evening the fishermen stowed their gear in preparation for a night's work. Fishing on the Sea of Galilee was an important industry and yielded a rich harvest, but it took long, hard hours, often until early morning. The gear consisted of different-size mesh nets, baskets to hold the catch, a stone anchor, torches for attracting fish, food and water jars, extra ropes and oars for propelling the boat.

The torches were made of staves or twigs bundled together to form a pocket in which to stuff a vegetable material soaked in pitch, wax, resin, or oil. The torches burned brightly enough to attract a catch as well as to provide light to work by on moonless nights.

Mending nets took up much of a fisherman's time when he was not actually fishing. The repairs were likely made on nets he had woven himself.

Gear and Tools of the Fisherman

The bronze barbed hooks shown below, along with cord and sinkers, were used in fishing. The larger multi-point hooks were attached to a short line, thrown into a shoal of fish and quickly snatched back, often snagging the flesh of fish for an easy catch.

The long bronze tools were used for repairing fine mesh nets. Like sewing needles they were threaded through the end hole and used to weave new cord into the damaged net.

The lead weights shown were used as sinkers on the perimeter of the nets.

Fishing villages like this one stretched along the shore of the Sea of Galilee. Simple, undressed basalt stone buildings with low, flat roofs flanked courtyards of various sizes. These small, "insula" type houses sheltered the poor fishermen and their families.

Nets dried on racks near the beached boats, and fishing gear and equipment were stored in courtyards already crowded with ovens, fireplaces, wood, and animals.

Fishing at night *was a common practice, employing torchlight to lure the fish to the surface and into the shallow dragnets. The drag-net could be secured to a buoy or between two boats that were steered in a circle to enclose the fish. The catch was then dragged into the boat and sorted. When the shoal of fish was found near the shore, one end of the net would be set in shallow water while the other end was taken out in a boat and pulled back to encircle the fish. The fish were then hauled ashore.*

A dragnet was not deep, but very long, often stretching hundreds of feet in length. In the water the net hung from floats and was held straight down by lead sinkers. When it was pulled in by long lines at both ends, it formed a bag that would hold the catch until it was hauled aboard.

A Rich Bounty

The Sea of Galilee, the Jordan River, and ponds yielded a harvest large enough to supply more than enough fresh fish for local needs; any extra from the catch went to the fishery for preserving.

Two kinds of fish were caught from these sources: the clean and the unclean. The "clean," which included the Tilapia (shown in the basket), and the Bleak or Lake Sardine, could be eaten by Jews. The "unclean" such as the catfish, eel, and lamprey, were immediately separated from the others and often sold to non-Jews.

Because of their abundance, fish were priced well within the means of the poorest and were often a mainstay in the daily diet of those living near the fresh waters of Palestine.

CHAPTER · EIGHT

To Earn One's Daily Bread

The people of first-century Palestine spent a large part of each day, much as we do today, working to earn their daily bread. They strongly believed that their creator wanted them to be diligent workers—working quietly for one's living was, by Jewish tradition, a duty and a sign of greatness.

What kinds of tasks did the workers of Jesus' time undertake to earn their living? What services did their crafts and trades provide? Where did they perform their work? What skills and tools did they use? And how were these occupations viewed by others?

As today, a person's occupation had a profound effect upon his character and the quality of his life and of the community. The New Testament and Talmudic literature provide us with a historical record of how the people of Jesus' time lived to labor and labored to live. The Jewish nation was known for its ingenuity and its many crafts and trade activities. Agriculture and industry were its strengths. Idleness was despised, if not condemned.

Many occupations that undoubtedly existed in New Testament times are not mentioned in the ancient writings. We may surmise that these vocations were so familiar that the authors saw no reason to discuss them.

This chapter deals with only a few occupations, mostly those with which the people of that day would likely have made daily contact. A few, such as that of the jailer, are included, not because they were generally known by the populace, but because they help give us a well-rounded picture of the times. Some of the most important and best-known occupations, such as those of the shepherd, farmer, potter, carpenter, and fisherman, have been treated separately and in more detail in other chapters

of this book. Many of the occupations illustrated differ somewhat from those we know today; some differ very little. Some of the trades and occupations that were important in ancient biblical times have not survived and are unfamiliar or unknown to us today.

Attitudes toward various occupations have changed markedly over the centuries. Today "blue-collar" jobs are viewed as inferior to other professions, but in the Palestine of the Gospels, manual labor and most crafts and trades were held in great esteem. A cursory review of biblical history shows that many of the great men of the Bible, even Jesus, earned their daily bread by common occupations. Saul, the first king of Israel, worked as a farmer and herdsman. David was a shepherd. Peter came from the fishing boat. Paul made tents, and Jesus entered his ministry after many years in a carpenter's workshop in Galilee. Most of the scholars of the day, the scribes and Pharisees, also worked with their hands at common trades for their daily support.

One of the important duties of a father of the day was to guide his son and apprentice him in an honorable occupation. Most often the son followed in the occupation of his father. Virtually every young Jewish man, whether rich or poor, was apprenticed to a craftsman to become skilled in a trade he could depend on for daily support—no matter what his vocation later in life. Even if he became a learned man, he would need a means of livelihood; he would need a skill.

The typical industries of the day were housed in the small, independent shops of the craftsmen. Here, in these privately owned workshops, the producers controlled quality and production and sold the products of their own hands directly to the consumer. A high value was attached to these handmade products, for skilled craftsmen were held in great esteem.

Those who practiced these skills tended to reside and work in their own districts and often formed local trade guilds. Guilds were organized for common social and economic benefits and served, as well, to protect the rights and secrets connected with the trade. Some of the larger guilds even had their own synagogues or bazaars, established in areas named after the trade: Baker Street, Fullers' Field, or Smiths' Bazaar.

In all ancient societies certain occupations were held in high esteem, but some trades were despised by the populace, and those who practiced these trades were disdained and often ostracized. Tradition attached low values to trades that were dirty, smelly, or unclean, as were those of the fuller or dyer. One trade, tanning, dealt with dead animals, and was declared unclean by Jewish law. Other occupations were notorious for dishonesty and unscrupulous conduct, fraud and deceit; innkeepers and tax collectors fell into this category.

The Jerusalem temple itself became one of the centers for trades and industry, for large numbers of specialized craftsmen were employed in building and restoring the complex. Many other skilled trades ensured the daily operation and provided the services of the temple. Great esteem and privilege accompanied work connected with the great temple, its maintenance or services.

The Jewish woman enjoyed a much higher status in the first century than most other women in the ancient world. She worked diligently rearing children, baking, cooking and providing for the many needs of her family: she often worked at other important jobs in the service of her community. In addition she may have worked in the paid employ of others, perhaps as a mourner or a servant.

It is difficult, if not impossible, to determine the wages paid to workmen, whether skilled or unskilled, esteemed or despised. We do know, in the only instance recorded in the New Testament, that the workman in a vineyard received a denarius for his day's labor, indicating that it had a reasonable buying power.

Most craftsmen and tradesmen of the day knew that honest work and a practiced skill brought their own rewards. Most men and women labored not merely for the daily wage received, or as a duty, but also to honor and obey their God and creator—the first worker.

■

The baker worked long and hard to provide "daily bread" for the many households that needed this basic food product. Many families baked their own bread in small neighborhood ovens or at home, while the baker produced large quantities for commercial sale. He would also receive loaves of dough from households to bake in his large hot oven, each loaf carefully imprinted with a distinctive mark for easy family identification.

The baker made bread from both wheat flour and barley meal, and always of the same size and weight. He prepared his fire in the evening and allowed it to burn throughout the night, thereby ensuring consistent oven heat for morning baking. The loaves would be baked upon heated stones which lined the bottom of the huge upper oven. In Jerusalem, small bakeries were established in an area called Baker Street.

For the beekeeper, *Palestine was truly a land flowing with honey. For centuries, honey had been the basic source of sweetening, but it was often limited to the quantities collected from wild hives between rocks and in hollow trees. The Romans, however, introduced an effective method of keeping domesticated bees: simple clay-pipe hives.*

The beekeeper would collect hives from the wild and put them in these clay pipes, placing the hives in orchards, which were good sources of pollen. The clay hives were blocked up, except for a slotted entrance, with a disc. When the beekeeper wanted to gather the honey, he burned dung near the entrance to drive out the swarm.

The barber *practiced his trade in the open air, usually in the shade of a building or tree. His tools were a razor, small shears, a few combs, and a mirror. He probably charged a very modest fee for his services.*

Most men had their hair trimmed to a reasonable length and shaved at the temples, as it was considered improper to have exceptionally long hair.

Bankers were important to the whole community,
but especially to the small craftsman. The bankers
provided services for exchanging currency, making
investments and extending loans. They took in money
for investments at small interest rates, and made
local, and even large international loans, at a much
higher rate of 8%. The wealthy invested their money
with bankers, while the unwise masses often buried
or hid it and did not collect interest.

Brickmaking was an ancient occupation. Especially where stone was
not readily available, sundried mud bricks have been widely used as a
common building material since earliest times.
    Bricks made from clay kneaded with straw and sand were molded
in wooden frames and set out in long rows to dry in the sun. Occasionally,
after being sundried, some bricks were put in a kiln and fired, making
them almost indestructible as a building material.

Involved in one of mankind's oldest occupations, the builder, *when inspired, could produce masterpieces, some unsurpassed even to this day. A builder was required to possess a thorough knowledge of all aspects of construction and organization, and often used Greek and Roman engineering and construction techniques. A builder's duties included supervising the actual day-to-day construction.*

Butchering was an important and necessary trade, as large and small communities alike required someone to slaughter and quarter animals for domestic consumption. Daily slaughter and small cuts were necessary because storage was not possible, so customers bought only that which would be immediately consumed. The butcher possessed considerable skill, knowledge, and manual dexterity in order to provide ritually clean meat, and to chop, saw, and cut up meat properly and safely.

The cheesemaker has, since ancient times, used milk from the cow, ewe, goat, and camel to produce cheese. Very early, man learned that milk allowed to stand in a warm place soon turned sour and formed a curd. Here the cheesemaker is separating the liquid whey from the solid curd.

In the time of Christ cheese was produced in large quantity for commercial sale by molding the curd into solid shapes. Cheese was popular because it could be preserved for long periods.

A cook was often employed in wealthy households to prepare the daily meals. He planned the menu, purchased the required foods, and supervised other kitchen workers engaged in the preparation and serving. In wealthy households which did not employ a full-time cook, professional cooks would be engaged for only special occasions and were probably well paid for their services.

The products of the coppersmith were loved throughout Palestine. The glow of the metal and the durability of the items made his shop a popular stop. Every piece was an individual work of art, done with the loving care of the craftsman.

To create his items he first heated and hammered the ingots of soft metal into thin sheets. These sheets were then repeatedly heated and stretched by pounding them over stakes of different shapes until the desired form was obtained. Spouts and handles could easily be attached by rivets to make a variety of personal and household products.

In Jerusalem, the cloth dyers were a
large and flourishing group. This practiced
trade had existed years before the time of
the Exodus, for we know that the covering
of the Tabernacle was dyed red. By the
first century, dyers could be found in most
centers throughout Palestine.

Using both animal and vegetable
dyes, the dyers' methods were simple,
messy, and smelly. Using the dipping
technique, it was the yarn that they colored,
before it was woven into cloth.

Fullers provided a service for both the cleaning and bleaching of older garments and the texturing and firming of new cloth. Since garments were valuable and had to last as long as possible, the work of the fuller was important in caring for personal garments. Used garments and new fabrics alike were steeped and trod in huge vats containing a water and alkaline mixture. New cloth would receive additional stamping and scraping. These fulling techniques created a foul odor, forcing fullers to locate their shops outside the towns. The need for water for washing and considerable space for drying the cloth in the sun or wind also determined the location of the fullers' shops.

Being a gardener was an occupation which brought beauty, color, and greenery to the drab environment of Palestine. The gardener worked hard at planting, cultivating, pruning, and gathering.

Gardens could be of many types and combinations: flower, vegetable, vine, or fruit. These gardens often provided a setting for graves and tombs.

The herdsman looked after herds of swine and did not enjoy a good reputation. He was despised partly because he was dishonest and repeatedly grazed his herd on the land of others, but mainly because his animals were an abomination, unclean, forbidden as food by Jewish law.

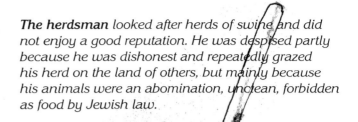

The hewer was usually a large man with big strong arms, as strength and stamina were required for working with stone. From the quarry walls he would cut huge stones to be used in constructing the buildings of Palestine.

By driving wooden wedges into pre-cut slots, the mammoth stones would be broken away in the required sizes. Only later would the stones be sized, squared, and shaped by the mason to fill specific needs.

Innkeepers provided lodging where travelers could find a haven and rest for the night. The public inns were generally unfurnished, dirty, badly managed and uncomfortable. Inns were designed to provide only the most elementary services—basically only shelter, food, and a stable for the animals. Innkeepers were known to be dishonest, immoral, and oppressive, especially to the many unsuspecting pilgrims en route to or from Jerusalem.

The jailer was often a retired soldier assigned to guard a prison, which was usually small and crude, and built in a fortress or tower. Depending on its purpose, a prison could have been a tiny detention area for mild restraint, a cold, damp cell, or a horrible dungeon. As a rule, if a prisoner escaped, the jailer was destined to suffer the same punishment as the prisoner.

Laborers were usually unskilled and very poor. They were numerous in Palestine. When they found work, which was infrequently, they would perform simple tasks such as sweeping streets and digging, doing field work, or loading and unloading. They hired out by the day, or even by the hour, and were likely to experience immediate hardship if work could not be found.

The merchant was either a local shopkeeper who sold goods each day in a specific location, or he was a traveling distributor who bought and sold goods as he moved between markets and countries.

Palestine was located on international trade routes and throughout the years benefited from the traveling merchants. By the first century, with an increase in population and broad Roman roads, goods from all over the world were available and the merchant's profits were high. He usually profited between 20% and 30%, and occasionally as much as 50% or even 100% on each sale.

Merchants, as a group, were considered dishonest because many employed crooked weights and measures.

Much as a smith does today, the metal worker *handcrafted custom items designed to fill specific customer needs. He also manufactured standard metal objects, including weapons, tools, and household utensils.*

In his furnace he could refine and alloy metal and then cast the molten metal into stone molds, to mass-produce items. When these castings cooled they would be further shaped, sharpened or polished to a finished state, depending upon their use. Using only hammer, anvil, furnace, and brawn, he forged the tools and implements for an advancing civilization. Some smiths plied their trade from place to place. In these smaller towns and villages they reshaped and repaired tools and implements.

The physician was consulted, as he is today, by the sick and infirm for dealing with the ills of the body. The Greek word for physician, ἰατρός, is related to ἰάομαι, meaning "to heal."

By the first century A.D., there had developed an extensive knowledge of natural medicines derived from minerals, herbs and plants. The medicinal use of these substances could relieve pain, clean wounds, or soothe aching bodies.

In the Roman world, sophisticated medical instruments were available for use in the highly developed art of surgery.

The shoemaker produced sandals which protected the feet against sharp and often hot stones. Sandals were made of leather, occasionally with wooden soles, and made to standard sizes. A person unable to afford a new pair had his sandals repaired by the shoemaker many times. Most peasants took great care of their sandals and wore them only when necessary.

Unlike sandals, shoes were worn mainly by the rich and only indoors, as much for fashion as for protection against the cold floors.

The stone mason, or "squarer," as he was often called, cut and dressed rough-quarried stone into finished construction stone. Since most public buildings were ornate, this highly skilled craftsman received many challenging opportunities. The skilled stone mason held a respected position among fellow craftsmen in his community.

The tanner, or leather worker, converted hides of goats, sheep, and camels into leather articles. This trade was considered repugnant because of the foul smell, and was despised because of the dead animals involved—which were unclean according to Jewish law.

The nature of the tanning process, as well as the need for much water, required the tanner's workshop to be a considerable distance, downwind and downstream, from any populous area.

In this illustration the tanner is scraping off the animal hair after the hide has been steeped in lime water. Later, the cleaned hide will be further soaked in a bark solution before being dried and trimmed.

The tax collector, or "publican," was responsible for collecting Roman taxes from his neighbors. The Roman government always farmed out this lucrative occupation to the highest bidder.

Tax collectors earned the contempt of their own people for extorting excessive taxes (they could demand and keep any extra taxes collected). The tax could be paid in coin or paid in goods. Despised by their people and considered akin to robbers and murderers, they were barred from many official and religious functions and often put on the same social level of a heathen slave.

The tent maker was a specialist in cutting and shaping fabrics for the making of tents. A coarse black sackcloth made from goat's hair was a favorite tent covering in the desert, while wool fabric or skins were generally used elsewhere. Making a tent was a laborious task, entailing cutting and sewing the cloth or leather panels into intricate tent shapes.

The occupations of women and the part these
occupations played in the community were very
significant by the first century. As well as fulfilling
the traditional women's role of the female in the
home, some women contributed to the economy of
the day as highly skilled and productive workers,
and by filling certain service needs of the community.
The following pages illustrate a few examples.

The midwife assisted a woman in labor, and at the actual birth helped
with the delivery, cut and tied the umbilical cord, and washed and swathed
the infant.

   Skilled midwives could also provide emergency medical or surgical
assistance if required, and were permitted to violate the injunctions against
work on the Sabbath when performing their duties. They acquired knowledge and skill from practical training with experienced midwives, and by
their own observation and experience. They sometimes assisted in the
delivery of domestic animals if complications arose.

Domestic servants were both men and women, usually skilled in all aspects of domestic life, typically of pleasant manner, faithful and hardworking.

Although service performed by the servant paralleled much of that done by a slave, the servant enjoyed higher status. He was a free individual, hired to perform specific duties for payment. A good domestic was usually treated with much respect and often considered a member of the family for which he or she worked. The death of the good servant was a greatly lamented loss.

The weaver's trade was considered the trade of women, although some men did work at the loom.

At this period, the textile industry was flourishing and production was increasing. The process of gathering and preparing fibers for weaving was usually carried out by other specialists.

The weavers illustrated are working on a horizontal loom, one of the common types used for weaving heavier fabrics. The second type was a vertical loom which was used to produce a finer wool or linen weave.

Professional wailers, or mourners, were those
hired to eulogize and bemoan the departed. They
were women who had mastered the art of mourning.
   Calculated to stir the emotions of bystanders
and those in the funeral procession, mourning would
include loud weeping and wailing, the playing of
flutes, beating the breast, wearing sackcloth, and
lamenting the dead with a wavering shrilled cry.
Even the poorest funeral was expected to have flute
players and at least one wailing woman.

CHAPTER · NINE

JERUSALEM: THE HOLY CITY

As he entered the city of Jerusalem through one of the dark, cool, massive gates in its northern wall, a first-century visitor would have been thrust instantly into a bright, sunlit marketplace. Through squinting eyes he would get his first close-up view of the splendor and grandeur of one of the great ancient cities. From afar, the many walls, massive structures and towers had presented the appearance of a gigantic, impregnable fortress that must have seemed, to our visitor, devoted to war rather than prayer, to security rather than pilgrimage.

By the time of Jesus, Jerusalem had been the holy place of Judaism for centuries. Inhabited as early as 1400 B.C., it had been a place of pilgrimage for the Jew through many of these years and had swelled enormously on the occasions of the great annual festivals. Pilgrims and travelers from every part of the Roman empire, and beyond, made their way then to this city of God.

When Jesus knew this city, the seeds of rebellion had already been planted that would produce a harvest of destruction for the inhabitants of this great city. This sacred city, the stronghold of Judaism, would soon be devastated.

As our visitor left the cool shadows of the northern gate, the sudden bright light and high-pitched activity in the gate market would have proved staggering. He probably moved quickly past the customs officials and through the busy marketplace into the bustling second quarter and its congested Tyropoeon Valley. This commercial area was the residence of the middle and upper-class shopkeepers, land owners and merchants; it was packed with homes, shops, restaurants and the workshops of master craftsmen.

On this major thoroughfare, with its endless movement of people, our visitor would have rubbed shoulders with many foreign visitors, Roman soldiers, wealthy people, priests, merchants, and pilgrims visiting from every known land. Most would have been moving past closely packed shops, while others would have been examining the inviting displays of quality goods from throughout the Roman world. Glass items of every description, fabric, colorful garments, jewelry, and brass and copper items would have flashed everywhere in the sun. Slowly our visitor would have made his way down the long valley street toward Herod's greatest achievement, the temple mount.

The Jewish temple and its complex was monumental. Its massive gates and splendid colonnades led to mammoth courts, of which the largest and most colorful was the Court of the Gentiles. Here he would have found the money-changers, hawkers of religious souvenirs, and sellers of sacrificial birds and animals. Beyond this court non-Jews dared not go, under penalty of death. The successive inner courts became progressively exclusive, and the sanctuary lying at the very heart of the complex was accessible only to the priests.

Throwing a long, dark shadow on the temple and its courts was the massive Fortress of Antonia. Situated in the northwest corner of the complex, this fortress was rebuilt by King Herod and named in honor of a Roman friend, Marc Antony. Its lofty towers were high enough to overlook the vast temple area if need arose, and it housed the Roman troops stationed in the city.

Directly south of the temple mount lay the original City of David. Sited on a narrow plateau, this old city had been completely walled-in by the first century, enclosing the magnificent palaces and homes of the wealthy and influential. From this vital area one could sense Jerusalem's history first hand.

Just below, in the Tyropoeon Valley, lay the city of the poor, the lower city. Packed with small limestone houses, and laced with narrow streets and alleyways, it extended to the Pool of Siloam in the southern extreme of the enclosed city, and to the temple mount and the second quarter in the northern portion. Here, congestion and squalor lay in the shadow of palaces and mansions standing conspicuously high upon both sides of this broad valley. In this lower city existed the many shops of Jerusalem's craftsmen.

Amid the small dull buildings on the valley floor, the magnificent hippodrome stood out in contrast. This was a stadium where young men strengthened their bodies and trained in the skills they exhibited in gladiatorial shows. North of the stadium, the valley narrowed as it passed under a major causeway that transported the rich and powerful of the upper city to the temple mount.

The broad Tyropoeon Valley formed a deep gash through the heart of the city with the temple mount and City of David on one side, the lower city in the valley itself, and the gleaming residential area of the upper city high upon the opposite, western side. In the upper city, as in the City of David, wealthy Jews and Romans lived in spacious white marble mansions on broad fashionable boulevards, comfortably removed from the rest of the city's population.

The beauty of the upper city provided a grand setting for the architectural magnificence of Herod's palace. Its occupants carried on their lavish lifestyle in royal splendor, in banquet halls and chambers large enough to accommodate hundreds. The setting for this citadel was one of huge pools and adorning spacious gardens with exotic trees and plants from all over the empire.

Directly in front of the palace was the Roman-style upper market, where fashionable and exotic goods were displayed in the vast open market, and specialty shops flourished in its arcades. Not far from the market, Herod's theater played Greek and Roman drama to packed houses.

Beyond the northern wall of the city, the newest suburb was growing by leaps and bounds. New residents, for want of space, had been forced to settle in the unwalled new city of Bezetha. Here a quiet open quarter of gardens, groves, and vineyards provided a dramatic contrast to the crowded Tyropoeon Valley and the splendor of the upper city. Bezetha was the last quarter to be enclosed within city walls, just before the destruction of the city by the Roman army in A.D. 70.

Jerusalem's new walls, as well as its old ones, gave way to Titus and his army as they systematically destroyed everything that was old or that Herod had built. The temple itself had just been completed after over eighty years of construction. After the city was razed in A.D. 70, it remained desolate, virtually uninhabited, for most of the century. All that was left of the magnificent holy city Jesus knew and loved was a Roman outpost on a city of rubble. ∎

Key to Jesus' Jerusalem

1. Temple
2. Viaduct
3. Xystus
4. Robinson's Arch
5. Hippodrome
6. Pool of Siloam
7. Solomon's Pool
8. Palace of Caiaphas
9. David's tomb
10. Herod's palace
11. Upper market
12. Theater
13. Palace of the Hasmoneans
14. Tower of Mariamme
15. Tower of Phasael
16. Tower of Hippicus
17. Golgotha Hill
18. Damascus Gate
19. Fortress of Antonia
20. Struthion Pool
21. Sheep pool
22. Pool of Israel
23. Golden Gate
24. Garden of Gethsemane
25. Absalom's tomb
26. Tomb of Zachariah

NOTE: This reconstruction of Jesus' Jerusalem is based, in part, on a model by Prof. M. Avi-Yonah of Hebrew University, Jerusalem.

© J. ROBERT TERINGO 1985

JERUSALEM
The City Jesus Knew

First-century Jerusalem was the city most visited and loved by Jesus and his followers. They knew its proud people; they visited its holy temple and courts, and walked through its mighty gates; they viewed its many magnificent buildings and strolled the narrow streets and broad causeways. In a few short years all would be gone—"not one stone here will be left on another; every one will be thrown down" (Matt. 24:2, NIV).

The pinnacle at the southeast corner of the temple mount was the highest spot in all Jerusalem.

The outer porticoes encircled the temple complex, adding much splendor to the mount. These porticoes served as a place for public assembly and for teaching. Dealers in ritual objects, as well as the temple money-changers, plied their trade in its halls.

The Fortress of Antonia stood on a huge, steep rock at the northwest corner of the temple mount and served as both fortress and barracks for the Roman garrison stationed in Jerusalem. Inside, it displayed much splendor in its halls, courts and baths. It featured high towers for overlooking the city and temple. If required, its soldiers could quickly descend by stairs from the towers to the temple porticoes, and then into the Court of the Gentiles.

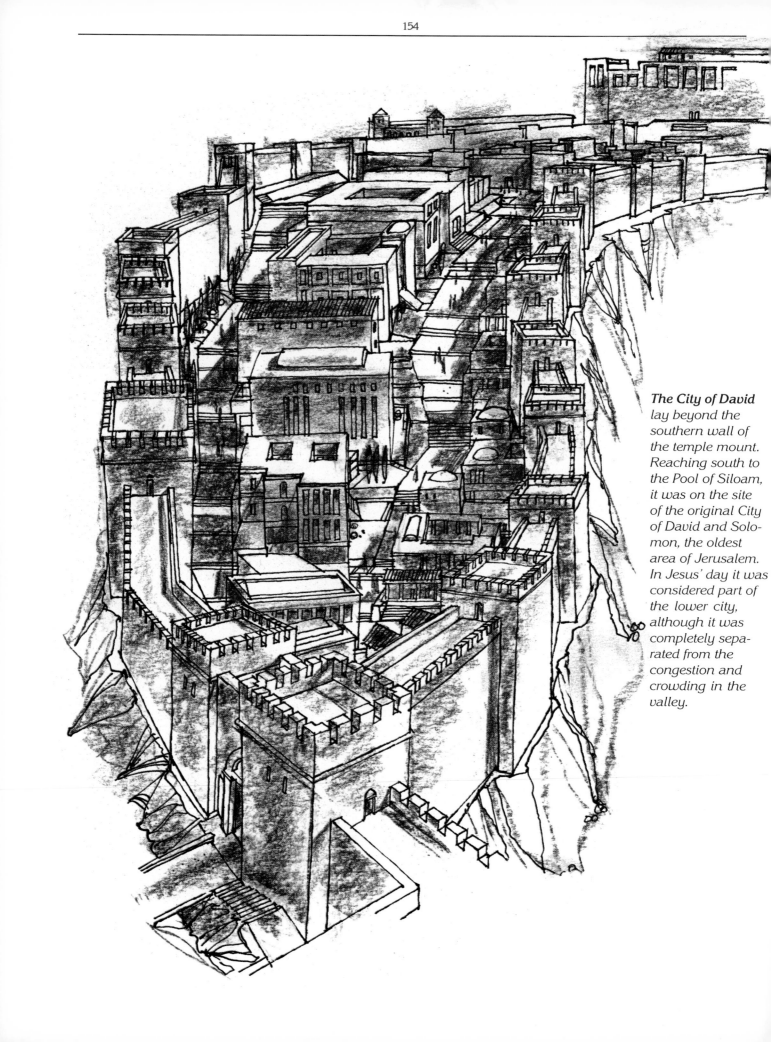

The City of David lay beyond the southern wall of the temple mount. Reaching south to the Pool of Siloam, it was on the site of the original City of David and Solomon, the oldest area of Jerusalem. In Jesus' day it was considered part of the lower city, although it was completely separated from the congestion and crowding in the valley.

Living in regal splendor were members of the old, established royal families, who desired to reside in the oldest and most famous Jewish section of Jerusalem. In great luxury they lived alongside many of the nation's wealthy merchants, landowners and bankers.

The Double Hulda Gate and Triple Hulda Gate were the well-known southern approaches to the temple mount and the Royal Portico. The gates were reached by wide stairs rising from the Ophel, the oldest part of ancient Jerusalem.

The densely populated lower city filled to capacity the southern part of the Tyropoeon Valley. Home to the poor and lower-class workers, this innermost city crowded the valley floor and slopes. Most buildings were of two-story, rough-cut stone construction, closely packed along narrow streets and alleyways. In every possible open area, neighborhood markets could be found. Oppressive dust, foul odors, and refuse intensified the discomforts of this crowded, densely populated quarter.

Robinson's Arch linked the temple mount to the Tyropoeon Valley. This arch supported a huge staircase which led from the lower city up into the temple courtyards. Situated just south of this temple corner was the hippodrome, a huge stadium built by Herod and devoted to games and sports.

The pool of Siloam, at the southern tip of the lower city, provided an abundance of water for the city. This man-made reservoir was where the sick and infirm were brought to bathe. The source of the sweet water was the Gihon Spring, which is connected to the pool by the ancient hand-hewn Hezekiah tunnel.

The workshops of Jerusalem's many craftsmen could be found in street-front shops among the lower city houses. Crowded together, each trade existed in its own section for the mutual benefit of its members.

The upper city lay before the great palace of Herod. The well-planned grid of streets and squares lent itself to the placement of magnificent villas and palaces, such as the home of Caiaphas, the High Priest.

Flanking the upper city on the north were three enormous towers built to protect the palace and named by Herod for his beloved wife, Mariamme; a friend, Hippicus; and a brother, Phasael.

The towers, along with other structures, such as King David's tomb and the theater, gave a predominantly Greek look to the upper city.

The upper market, with
its arcade of fine shops,
provided a Roman-style open
market where imported luxury goods could be
purchased. In the illustration
a wealthy family shops,
while a slave girl carries a
basket of exotic fruit for her
owners.

Herod's great palace was built on the highest, westernmost terrace in the upper city, directly across the broad Tyropoeon Valley from the temple. A fortress as well as a palace, it overlooked the entire city.

Built on a raised foundation, the palace was surrounded by a stout, towered wall. Inside the wall were groves and gardens with huge bronze figures from which water poured. Surrounding the palace were circular porticoes and walkways, bordered by canals and gardens containing exotic plants and animals.

The palace itself was a magnificent structure, with extended wings

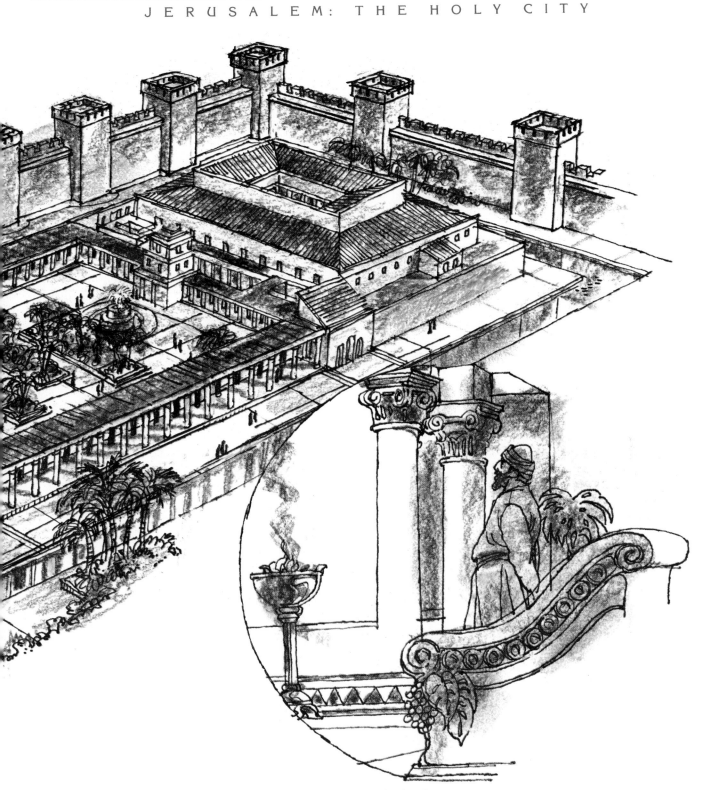

that contained halls and bedrooms to accommodate hundreds of guests.
Rare stone was used in abundance; halls were supported by huge ceiling
beams of exotic woods; and everywhere there was great splendor in the
adornments. Its apartments were beautifully furnished and appointed
in gold and silver. The beauty of the palace was unsurpassed anywhere in
Palestine.

   In Herod's time the palace complex was the headquarters from
which he ruled. By Jesus' day it had become the temporary seat of the
Roman government when the procurator stayed in Jerusalem.

Luxury goods from all over the Roman world could be found in the second quarter shops. The examples illustrated represent only a small selection of the goods available. Glass bottles and jugs were very popular, as were such metal items as a hand mirror, thimble or scissors. Furniture, such as the Roman-style couch shown, would have been in great demand.

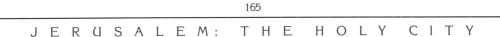

The Tyropoeon Valley of the second quarter was where the upper and middle classes lived and shopped. Lining the wide valley roads were enclosed shops selling a variety of luxury goods to this affluent neighborhood.

The market at the Damascus Gate was the largest and most popular marketplace in the second quarter. Here, in one vast open market, most daily food and household needs could be purchased.

Outside the city, quiet gardens, groves, and farmland contrasted with the crowded city. As the city's population increased, and lack of space forced new residents and businesses to locate elsewhere, many new villas were also built outside the walled city.

The wood market and numerous storage facilities could be found just outside the northern gates. The sheep pool, a public bathing place, a sheep market, and the monument of Alexander Jannaeus lay north of the temple mount. Various tombs, including the tomb of Absolom, could be found in the Kidron Valley east of the temple. Beyond the valley was the beautiful Garden of Gethsemane.

CHAPTER·TEN

THE PEOPLE OF THE LAW

"Hear, O Israel: The Lord our God, the Lord is one" (Deut. 6:4, NIV). Throughout the centuries, the Jews had rallied to this ancient command with an absolute and uncompromising faith. They were God's chosen people, and the pride of belonging to a special covenant with God rested in their hearts. If they would worship him as their forefathers had and would obey his commands, the covenant promised his blessing. This conviction made obedience to God's laws the objective of their daily lives. By the first century, the innermost feelings of the Jew in Palestine could be summed up simply: love of, and devotion to, the laws of God, accompanied by an intense hatred for foreign domination and its cultural influence.

In 63 B.C., the powerful Romans, under Pompey, took Jerusalem and abruptly ended Jewish religious and political freedom. By the first century, Jewish Palestine had (in theory) been restored to a theocracy, meaning the law of God was also the law of the land. In reality it was an occupied country with little power of its own. Jewish leadership was in the hands of the high priest, whose power, although restricted to the Jewish world, extended into religious, political and administrative realms.

Since early times, the high priest and the Jewish priesthood had taken an important place in the daily religious lives of the people. The priests were the guardians of the temple and its worship, and they represented the people in presenting offerings of sacrifices at the altar of God in Jerusalem.

Many Jewish religious sects and parties thrived in Jesus' day, but the two most prominent were the Pharisees and the Saddu-cees. As a priestly class of temple leaders, the Sadducees held much of the power, while the Pharisees, because of their popularity and their knowledge of Jewish law, held a position of great influence among the people. Other sects included the Essenes, who removed themselves from the social system to live an isolated life in remote spots, and the extremist Zealots, who became political rebels.

A major group within the Pharisees, who were expert in the interpretation of the law, was known as scribes. Although not all scribes were Pharisees, all scribes were devoted to the law of God, living in and for the law.

The Sanhedrin, or high court of the Jews, was composed of two diametrically opposed factions: the aristocratic and wealthy Sadducees and the popular Pharisees. The Sadducees held the power in the court, but the Pharisees were allowed to participate because of their popular support. The Sanhedrin was charged with administering and interpreting the law of God in the daily lives of all the Jewish people, not only of those living in Palestine proper, but also of those living in the Jewish colonies of the Diaspora (Jews exiled in earlier foreign invasions). Occasionally, this court was itself divided about those interpretations.

There were many special and sacred days in the Jewish life of the first century. The Sabbath, the most important of these, was observed on the last day of each week as a day of worship set aside that God's people might rest from their labors and be refreshed. The festivals of Pentecost, Passover, and the Feast of Tabernacles were sacred days that were observed annually. These festivals were instituted to commemorate the goodness and blessings received from the Creator. Festivals served to bind the Jewish nation and were celebrated in every Jewish home with much feasting, prayer and sacrifice. The Day of

Atonement drew great crowds of the faithful from every part of the Roman world to the temple in Jerusalem, to witness a sacred ritual of the high priest.

In addition to the temple, during the centuries before and during Jesus' day, the synagogue was extremely important in the daily lives of all Jews, no matter where they lived. It was, in part, the physical separation from the temple in Jerusalem that gave birth to this institution. First and foremost, the synagogue was a house of prayer and the place where the law was read and studied. It was also a school where the community, especially children, were educated in the law, and the customs and traditions of their forefathers. As the focus of the community, the synagogue often served other functions as well—as a town hall, community center, lodging place for travelers and, occasionally, as a courtroom.

The period before the destruction of the temple proved difficult and frustrating for those Jews living in Palestine. Life was as harsh as ever, Roman taxes were high, and the quality of their daily life was deteriorating. Even their religious world was not exempt, for through these years, as the people struggled to maintain order and give meaning to their lives, new religious orders and sects arose. Some sects withdrew into the desert with hope for a life of devotion and purity, while other overly zealous groups became right-wing rebels, developing later into terrorists and assassins. These activist Zealots believed that the perfect Jewish state would come only through the elimination of all authority except God's.

During these difficult times a seed was planted, only to die, but from its death a new growth sprang up from the fertile soil. The seedling would become the spreading tree of Christianity, a new order clashing sharply with Judaism and its traditions. At first called Nazarenes, and later Christians, its adherents throughout the Roman world would be ostracized and persecuted for their beliefs; but the growth would spread across the land Jesus knew and loved, finally to put roots deep into the Roman world. ∎

The Pharisees were a popular sect with great authority and influence over the Jews of first-century Palestine. Since most Pharisees were themselves of the middle class, they were trusted by the people.

The Pharisees were revered because their precise knowledge of the law of Moses, made them seem more acceptable to God. People believed that this knowledge made them the custodians of the oral clarification of that law, in interpretations that had been handed down from generations. These traditions were fundamental principles which they followed with absolute respect.

Pharisees held high positions in the community and were members of the high Jewish court, the Sanhedrin. Many Pharisees were so knowledgeable in the law that they became scribes or, as they were also known, lawyers, and doctors of the law.

Scribes, or lawyers, were interchangeable titles for men learned in the law. The scribes served as interpreters and teachers of that law, as well as recorders in meetings of the Sanhedrin.

Most scribes, but not all, were of the party of the Pharisees. Most were devoted, first and foremost, to the law and its interpretation.

The Sadducees were a priestly sect composed of men of wealth and power. This party controlled the priesthood, the temple, and its operation and immense wealth. At times they also dominated the high court of the Jews, the Sanhedrin.

The Sadducees were fundamentalists in their approach to the law of Moses—they accepted only the written law and not the oral traditions of the Pharisees which had grown up around that law. Their ideas did not always appeal to the masses, and often had little support from the middle and lower classes. The Sadducees were obligated, because of their lack of public support, to allow the Pharisees to participate in religious as well as secular affairs. When the temple was destroyed by the Romans, the Sadducees disappeared with it, as their influence and priestly functions were no longer required.

The priesthood was the heart of temple activity, for the priests served as mediators between the people and their God. At the head of the priesthood stood the ultimate authority, the high priest, the very symbol of the Jewish religion. His tenure as high priest was for life, but in reality he could be, and was often, deposed, especially if he failed to meet the political expectations of Roman rule.

As guardians of the temple worship, considerable numbers of priests were required in Jerusalem each week to support the intricate ceremonial system. Divided into twenty-four classes, each class officiated, in turn, for one full week. Called from throughout Palestine, they came to perform their assigned duties in the temple services.

The vestments of the priest consisted of four simple garments. Next to the body he wore white linen drawers. Over this undergarment was a tunic of white checkered linen, and over the white tunic he wore a colorfully embroidered girdle made of cords wound many times around the waist and tied. The ends hung to the ground. On his head he wore a white linen headpiece.

The high priest wore the same four vestments, but to them he added his "golden vestments": the blue sleeveless robe with golden bells; the colorful ephod apron worn over the robe; and a breastplate of twelve precious stones. On his head he wore a white linen miter, and, covering the forehead, a golden plate bearing the inscription "Holy to the Lord."

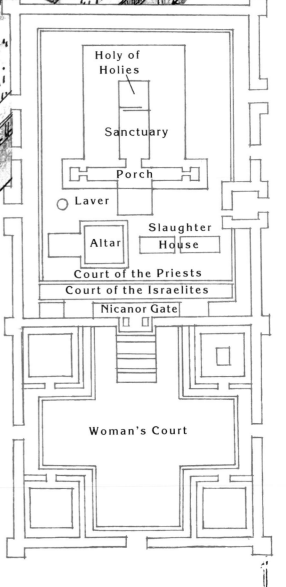

The Second Temple

The second temple complex consisted of a series of successive enclosures, through which one passed to reach the sacred Sanctuary. Located on a mount between two deep valleys to the east and west, the complex was protected on the north by the massive Fortress of Antonia, and on the south by the City of David.

To clearly understand the complex and its religious meaning, we must look at the circled degrees of holiness which surrounded this house of God. The land of Palestine was the largest circle. Inside this was the province of Judea around the city of Jerusalem, with the temple mount centered in the city. Within this complex the first, and outermost, enclosure was the Court of the Gentiles. Inside the temple itself, the next level was the Woman's Court, then on through the Nicanor Gate into the narrow Court of Israel. Within the Court of Priests, beyond the altar, the laver, and the slaughter house, stood the Sanctuary. Proceeding up the steps to the Porch, and into the Sanctuary itself, we go then to the final and most sacred spot of all, the Holy of Holies.

Once within the walls of the temple complex, one would have been awed by its size, its beauty, and the vast activity in its courts. Beyond the first court, the activities were limited to all but the Jews. At the entrance to the inner courts, inscriptions in Hebrew, Latin, and Greek warned that under penalty of death no further entrance could be made by Gentile or unclean Jew.

The immense court of the Gentiles was situated
in the outermost part of the temple mount and lay
nearly fifty feet lower than the temple itself. This
great expanse entirely enclosed the temple and its
higher courts. The court of the Gentiles was itself
enclosed by colonnades of unsurpassed magnificence.

In this open expanse, its longest side, nearly
250 yards longs, one would have found the sellers of
sacrificial animals, and the busy money-changers
selling temple coinage to pilgrims. Within the beautiful
porticoes, out of the sun and rain, teachers could be
heard preaching and lawyers could be heard arguing
over the fine points of the law.

There were always crowds of visitors, both Jew
and Gentile, many from distant lands, in this public
place. Huge gates breached the formidable walls
of the temple mount allowing easy access from the
city on the west, and from the countryside on the
east.

The courts of the temple represented degrees of holiness surrounding the most sacred Holy of Holies. The temple complex was separated into terraced courts, each higher and more exclusive as one approached the Sanctuary.

After the outer court of the Gentiles, the inner courts were available only to ritually clean Jews. The Woman's Court visualized here was impressive in size, yet much smaller and more intimate than the larger outer court. A chamber protruded from each corner, but the focus of the court was the massive Nicanor Gate. Stairs led through the huge bronze gate into the Court of Israel, behind which lay the Court of Priests. Women were excluded from these courts, so the gate provided them the only view of the temple and its altar.

The temple complex represented different things to different people. To the Jews, the temple was the house of the living God, the place for prayer and sacrifice. To others, the outer courts of the complex were a meeting place, a place where Jew and Gentile rubbed shoulders. To some, the temple was a popular tourist area where travelers from throughout the world came to view the splendors of this great structure.

The colonnades served as a school where one could learn from the many impromptu discussions and lectures. The outer court housed a commercial center where foreign monies could be exchanged into the currency of the temple, or where items required for sacrifice, and even temple souvenirs, could be purchased.

If all visitors could have entered the restricted inner courts, they would have seen in the Court of Priests an area in which sacrificial animals were prepared, an area that resembled a literal slaughter house.

The Levites—Servants at the Temple

The name Levite was used for those Jews of the tribe of Levi. Although Levites were engaged in the temple service, they did not look after priestly matters and were denied any priestly connection with the altar and its sacrifices.

Although on the permanent staff at the temple, the Levites were considered to be only servants at the complex. They were engaged in all types of support functions as administrators, singers and musicians, and gatekeepers, and performed the major housekeeping and policing duties as well. By the first century the Levites had lost much of their earlier status and were looked upon as members of a secondary group in the heirarchy.

The fixed order of service began, after the customary greeting, with a prayer while the people remained standing facing the sacred Torah scroll. The reading of the law of Moses was next. The Torah scroll was taken from the chest and placed before a reader who read in the ancient Hebrew tongue and immediately translated it into Aramaic, the language of those days. A commentary was always added to this reading.

Next, a portion was read from the books of the prophets and, again, immediately translated verse by verse. After a closing prayer, the service was concluded, except for a possible collection on weekdays to aid the poor.

The scroll was a book, written on specially-prepared parchment, animal skins or papyrus. These sheets of handwritten text in ink, were sewn together to make a long strip and then rolled around a stick. Because Hebrew and Aramaic are read right to left, back-to-front in our modern book form, the scroll was unwound off the left hand roll and wound into the right hand. Scrolls were copied by dedicated professional scribes and were stored in cloth cases, jars, racks or wooden chests.

THE PEOPLE OF THE LAW

The synagogue was a house of God, established as a place for prayer and the reading and study of the law of Moses.

Prayers and instruction in the synagogue had a great influence on the daily lives of the people of Palestine. This influence gave meaning to their lives, making the synagogue very different from the temple in Jerusalem. In the temple the focus had been on the sacrifice, through the priests, as the main interaction of the people with God. With study and prayers at their local synagogues available to them, however, the people no longer felt dependent on the distant temple for maintaining a relationship with their God.

In all the synagogues of Palestine, and in Jewish communities throughout the world, the same kind of organized congregation and established order of service existed. The synagogue was open daily for prayer. On the Sabbath, the entire Jewish community came for prayer and to learn from the law and the prophets. Learned persons or congregational elders read lessons and gave comments. Exclusion from these services was considered a very great punishment.

In addition to being a house of prayer, the synagogue also served as a community center, a school, a lodging place for travelers, and occasionally as a court for hearing civil cases. It was truly the focal point of the community.

Elders were the duly-appointed officers of the synagogue, chosen by the people from among the learned and respected members of the community. The elders, with one serving as president, presided over the assembly and the synagogue school. It was through the synagogue that the general needs of the community were administered.

The Day of Atonement (Yom Kippur) came on the tenth day of Tishri (September-October), five days before the Festival of Sukkot—Tabernacles. This major festival was a day of fasting and solemn prayers of atonement for sins against God. On this, the holiest day of the year, the masses assembled at the temple to witness the sacred ritual as the high priest ministered in the Sanctuary and then entered into the Holy of Holies.

On the previous day, in preparation for his entry, the high priest was separated from others in a special room to avoid ritual uncleanness. At the service he was given a ladle and firepan, with a measure of incense in the ladle. He went through the Sanctuary to the two veils separating the Holy of Holies from the Sanctuary; there he entered on the left end of the outer veil. Then he proceeded between the two until he reached the other end, drew aside the inside veil and entered the holy chamber.

Once inside he poured the incense on burning coals in the firepan he had placed upon the foundation stone in the center of the floor. The chamber quickly filled with smoke from the incense as he prayed. When finished he came out as he had entered.

The Feast of Tabernacles (Sukkot) was a festival of splendor and thanksgiving. In honor of the vintage and harvest of the first fruits, this extremely joyous festival signaled the close of the agricultural labors of the season. To show recognition for God's bounty, the choicest of the first fruits were displayed and carried about for everyone to see.

Rejoicing began at sunset of the first day of the week-long festival, when people danced in the temple courts by the light of torches and bonfires. They virtually took possession of the temple at this festival and participated equally with the priests in most of their festive duties.

This feast also commemorated Israel's wilderness wandering. Celebrants would construct booths in which they lived during the feast, to recall their ancestors' forty-year life in temporary dwellings.

Passover (Pesah) was instituted to preserve the memory of the liberation of the early Israelites from Egyptian bondage. The festival was so-named because the God of the Israelites passed over their houses when he destroyed the firstborn of Egypt. To commemorate the exodus of their forefathers under Moses, the Jews ate unleavened bread during the entire Paschal week, and roasted a kid or lamb for the Passover meal.

Shortly after being slain, the blood of the animals was sprinkled upon the great altar at the temple, whereas at the original event the blood was sprinkled upon the doorpost so that the "angel of death" would pass by. The Passover feast began on the fifteenth of Nissan (March-April) and continued to the twenty-first. It was one of the most important and festive of all Jewish celebrations.

The Sabbath, or day of rest, *began at sunset on Friday with the blowing of the shofar (ram's horn) and closed with a benediction at sunset on Saturday, the seventh day. This special day was reserved to acknowledge symbolically that God was the creator of the universe and that only He was worthy of worship. The Sabbath was instituted at creation so that man might rest from his work and be refreshed and rejoice in God's goodness. It was also a day of prayer.*

Pentecost (Shavuot), *or Feast of Weeks was a festival of thanksgiving held at the close of the grain harvest, fifty days after Passover. Everyone brought an offering to God the provider, according to blessings received.*

Loaves of bread, made of fine flour from grain gathered at harvest, were among the first fruits presented in gratefulness for the bountiful crops. Many Jews from foreign countries came home to Jerusalem for this joyous festival.

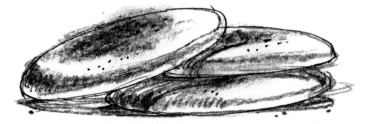

The Key to the Synagogue

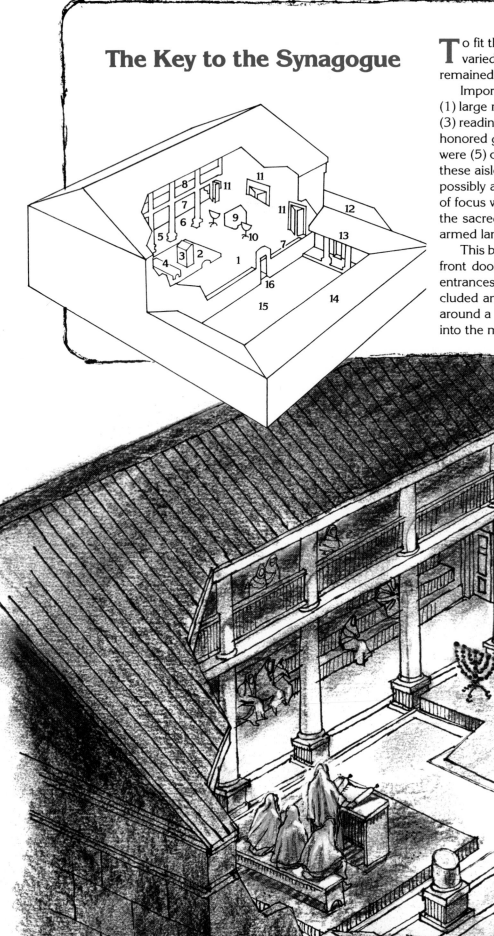

To fit the needs of the community the buildings varied in size and style, although many main features remained the same.

Important aspects of the synagogue included its (1) large reading room and (2) raised platform, with a (3) reading table and (4) choice seats for the elders and honored guests. Often, around the large main room, were (5) columns, (6) aisles and (7) benches. Above these aisles was often built a (8) second-story balcony, possibly a place for the women to worship. The center of focus was the (9) ark, a portable chest for holding the sacred Torah scrolls, and (10) *menorahs,* seven-armed lampstands.

This building was entered through (11) three front doors—one main door and two small entrances off the (12) porch. The structure often included an (13) outside entrance to (14) chambers around a (15) paved courtyard with a (16) side entrance into the main reading room.

The synagogue school provided the only formal education available. Under a qualified schoolmaster, boys received their education studying the Scriptures at the feet of a teacher, learning to read and recite much of it in sing-song fashion. The synagogue school passed on to children the traditions and spiritual heritage of their forefathers.

The classic synagogue was rectangular, often with an attached courtyard and chambers. Its interior was usually a large reading room with benches, and it often had a second story with a balcony. The building customarily faced Jerusalem, and was erected on the highest possible location. As worshipers entered they turned to face both the ark and Jerusalem. Some scholars have suggested that before the destruction of the temple in A.D. 70, synagogues were built facing east, as the temple itself, and not till later in the first century were they oriented to face the missing temple. The average synagogue was probably smaller and less elaborate than the one illustrated.

The Essenes *lived in the isolated community of Qumran, on the western shore of the Dead Sea. Here scribes copied ancient Hebrew scriptures and wrote other works, including a manual of discipline. Because these writings were stored in clay jars in a dry climate, they survived and are known today as the Dead Sea Scrolls.*

Jews by birth, the Essenes had great affection for their religious brethren. They lived simple lives of poverty, celibacy and obedience, rejecting worldly pleasures and riches. Because they shared everything in common, no man among them had more material goods than another. The final fate of this religious sect is unknown, but we do know the Romans overran the large community of Qumran in A.D. 68.

The Zealot and the Samaritan

The Zealots were right-wing extremists—often activists, terrorists and assassins who believed that the kingdom of God could be established by force. They continually stirred up the passions of the people against those who had authority, especially foreigners, and anyone who recognized that authority.

The Zealots' religious beliefs were similar to those of the Pharisees. In fact, they had emerged from that body, but, unlike their former associates, they acknowledged no master but God. As activists, the Zealots gained the support of the masses for sporadic bloody uprisings against Roman rule. They were finally destroyed at Jerusalem and Masada, in the war with Rome.

For many years the Samaritans were socially despised by their Jewish neighbors. Because of long-standing religious and political ill-feelings, there were few dealings between the Samaritans and the other Jews of Palestine. As an example of the controversy, the Samaritans did not accept all the books of the Old Testament as holy, nor did they consider the temple in Jerusalem the proper place to worship and sacrifice.

Although the Samaritans accepted the faith of the Jew, or at least most of its tenets, and had all the legal rights and privileges of any Jew, they were despised even more than the Gentile. To be called a Samaritan was one of the lowest forms of abuse one Jew could bestow upon another.

The lives of the early Christian disciples reflected their conviction that they were continuing the special mission Jesus had assigned them. They traveled from town to town proclaiming the "good news" in their preaching.

These disciples of Jesus often preached to the masses out-of-doors in the open countryside near the Sea of Galilee. As most of the Jews in Jesus' time were familiar with the promises of the Old Testament, the disciples explained their conviction that Jesus fulfilled many of these promises, especially those foretelling a messiah.

Few, in that day, realized that this small band of "Nazarenes" was more than just another Jewish religious sect, one of the many appearing in those turbulent times. What was in fact emerging was a new order, an order that would become a worldwide religion—Christianity.

In a missionary spirit, the disciples of Jesus carried the gospel to all who would listen. Wherever they went, to the Jews of Palestine or the Gentiles in other parts of the Roman world, small congregations would assemble for study and prayer. These inspired Christians were holding meetings to teach the young and old alike the new ways, sometimes in the local established synagogues, but especially in the private homes of their brethren. These were the first church services of Christendom.

In every village and town, the sick and crippled would gather around the disciples of Jesus, hoping to be healed. God worked many miracles through these dedicated men, not only restoring the sick, but even raising the dead.

Phylacteries *were small cases which enabled one to carry on his person selected portions of the law. They served as a reminder of the love of God and His commandments. Some pious men wore them at all times, but most wore them only during prayers.*

There were two kinds of phylacteries, the frontlet, which was worn on the head, and one which was worn on the arm. A calfskin case holding rolls of parchment scriptures was tied to the upper arm just above the elbow, with the straps continuing around the arm and fingers. The frontlet also had a case holding scriptures, but was tied to the head and rested on the forehead.

Music and song *have always played an important part in the lives of the Jewish people. Whether by the simple tune of the shepherd's pipe, or by the ceremonial music of the temple musicians, their secular and religious activities were accompanied by music.*

At the temple, musicians played cymbals and stringed instruments, such as the harp, while silver trumpets signaled the commencement of activities. Few ancient nations used music as extensively as did these people in their everyday activities.

The sacrifice, to the Jew, was the act of ceremonially offering a substitute to God which was burned or poured out, to atone for one's sins.

According to the law of Moses, sacrificial offerings could only be made on the altar at the temple. Unblemished clean animals, such as the ox, sheep or goat, and even birds, such as the pigeon or turtledove, were acceptable offerings. The law dictated the offering required, but the financial ability of the worshiper to provide it determined the kind of animal.

In the animal sacrifice, the first act of "laying on of the hands" belonged to the one making the presentation, while the slaying, skinning, flailing, sprinkling of the blood, and the laying of the pieces on the altar were priestly functions.

For a bloodless offering, wine, fine flour, or oil was acceptable. From the flour, dough could be made and baked into cakes, loaves or wafers, all equally acceptable. Salt was the symbol of incorruption and was added to all offerings, both bloodless and blood sacrifices.

The Jewish Calendar

Unlike other calendars, which are based upon the earth's revolution around the sun, the Jewish calendar was calculated by the phases of the moon. This lunar calendar had 354 days, with approximately every third year requiring an additional month. On a leap year, the entire new month of Adar II ("Adar Sheni") was inserted into the calendar following the regular 12th month of Adar.

Depending upon the new moon, each month consisted of either 29 or 30 days. Serving as the basis for establishing the end and beginning of the month, the new moon also determined the proper days for religious observances. No year was to have fewer than four, nor more than eight, full months of thirty days.

The Jewish day was divided into twelve hours, the night into three watches. Generally, the first hour of the day corresponded to our 6 a.m. and the sixth hour to our noon. The day came to a close at 6 p.m. or upon sunset. (The Romans began their day, or first hour, at midnight, which explains the difference between times of the day.) The length of the day varied greatly depending upon the season, with the longest day of the year being over fourteen hours.

In addition to the following observances, every seventh day, the Sabbath, was a festival day.

Month	Festival Days	Month	Festival Days
NISSAN March–April	1 New Moon's Day 14 Passover (*Pesah*) and Paschal Sacrifice 15 The Feast of Unleavened Bread 16 Presentation of the Omer 21 Close of Passover and the Feast of Unleavened Bread	TISHRI September–October	1 New Year's Feast (*Rosh Hashanah*) or Feast of Trumpets 2 New Year's Feast 3 Fast in memory of the murder of Gedaliah 10 Day of Atonement (*Yom Kippur*) or The Great Fast 15 Feast of Tabernacles (*Sukkot*) 21 Close of the Feast of Tabernacles 22 *Shmini Atzeret*, the 8th day following the Feast of Tabernacles
IYAR April–May	1 New Moon's Day 14 Second Passover (Kept by those who had been unable to observe the first) 18 *Lag B'Omer*, or the Scholar's Feast		
SIVAN May–June	1 New Moon's Day 6 Pentecost (*Shavuot*) or Feast of Weeks	CHESHVAN October–November	1 New Moon's Day
TAMMUZ June–July	1 New Moon's Day 17 Fast to commemorate the loss of Jerusalem to Nebuchadnezzar (if the 17th occurs on the Sabbath, the fast is kept on the 18th)	KISLEV November–December	1 New Moon's Day 25 Hanukkah, or Feast of Lights, to commemorate the rededication of the temple (8 Days)
AV July–August	1 New Moon's Day 9 Fast to commemorate the destruction of the first temple 15 The Feast of Wood (offering)	TEVET December–January	1 New Moon's Day 10 Fast to commemorate the siege of Jerusalem
		SHEVAT January–February	1 New Moon's Day 15 *Tu B'Shevat*, the New Year of the Trees
ELUL August–September (always 29 days)	7 New Moon's Day	ADAR February–March	1 New Moon's Day 13 Fast of Esther (if it falls on the Sabbath, it is to be kept on the preceding Thursday) 14 Feast of *Purim* 15 *Purim* (alternate date)

CHAPTER·ELEVEN

THE CUSTOMS OF THE DAY

The real character of a people and its culture can best be appreciated if one studies their manner and customs. In Bible lands, for example, a host felt it his sacred duty to protect those whom he received into his home to eat with him—even a crust of bread—and defend them, if necessary, to the death.

This custom of friendship and hospitality was characteristic of the duty felt of those of the East, and tells us much about the times, and more importantly, what was in their minds and in their hearts.

In every culture and every age, there are established forms of conduct, manners considered appropriate for successful interaction with family, community, and in religious observances. The Jews of first-century Palestine were no exception. They lived with a vast network of customs and traditions—requirements that fixed the framework of their religious life and directed every aspect of their daily lives.

In Jesus' day the Jews followed many customs that differ greatly from those we observe in Western culture today. For example: We sit down to eat, but they reclined; our houses look out, but in Palestine, all but the smallest one-room houses faced inward; we may go out for a breath of fresh air or a walk, but they went into the courtyard or up to the roof for air.

One of the striking traits of most Jews in first-century Palestine was the stubbornness they exhibited in following the ways of past generations. The customs and manners of their ancestors were used as a guide for the proper life.

Not all the manners and customs of Jesus' time can be illustrated within the limited space of this book, but a selected few may give a sense of those customs in Palestine with which Jesus and the early Christians would have been well acquainted. They used many of these to illustrate their stories.

The family unit was the cornerstone of Jewish life in Palestine; one's flesh and blood was an exceedingly important part of the world in which one lived. Through the family most customs were handed down, and when these established traditions were faithfully upheld, the family was a stronger social and religious unit.

The father, or elder, was the key to a strong unit, and held great power over the family. When he died the family name and unity were carried on through the eldest son, the firstborn. If the family was fortunate enough to have many sons, it would grow and prosper as the young families of married sons joined the existing family unit. Only occasionally did sons go off and begin their own units. This explains the great joy of the parents upon the birth of every son.

The institution of marriage also played an important role within Judaism. Marriage was governed by strict legal and religious requirements, as well as by customs that had been practiced for centuries. The family head usually selected the wife for his son and the husband for his daughter. In each case, the families made an agreement which covered, among other things, the dowry to be given for the bride. This contract sealed the engagement and was considered final, fulfilling the legal requirements.

After this ceremony of betrothal, the bride might go directly to the home of the bridegroom. Ordinarily, however, she remained in her father's house for as long as a year during this period of engagement, often with little or no contact with the bridegroom. Legally, only death or divorce could separate the betrothed. The marriage was consummated when the bride left her father's house to live in the home of the bridegroom.

Throughout the centuries, Jews in Palestine voluntarily practiced hospitality toward almost anyone in need of it, considering it a highly honorable act. In Jesus' time, because of Palestine's occupation by foreigners, hospitality toward outsiders, especially Gentiles, became less common.

Every ancient culture had peculiarities of manner and a specified civility that guided politeness when interacting with one's neighbors. In first-century Palestine many of these acts of politeness would have, by our standards, seemed extravagant and excessive—for example: prostrating oneself on the ground before another, or addressing one as "My Lord," when one's true feelings could have been shown by a moderate nod of the head, or simply a polite word.

Burial of the dead involved many different ceremonies in the varied lands of the Bible, but without exception it was considered a sign of great contempt to deprive the dead of a proper burial.

Imitating the ancient Persians, the Jews of Palestine customarily buried their dead very soon after death, even on the same day if possible. Upon death the body was immediately prepared for burial, placed upon a bier and carried to a tomb for interment. The mourners followed, pouring forth the sadness in their hearts with shrieking and weeping. Departed men of rank, who were considered favored and loved by the people, would be honored by the attendance of vast multitudes. It was the common custom for the family and close friends to visit the tomb site after the burial to continue their expression of grief and loss. With great lamentation, the mourning would go on for days.

Two very strong pressures, Graeco-Roman culture and Judaic traditionalism, were working at the time of Jesus, and would alter many of their ancient manners and customs. The first century was a world of ferment, a time when two diverse civilizations came into conflict. Many believed that the greatest of these pressures were the thoughts and ideals of Graeco-Roman culture. This culture represented an alternative way of life, and attracted those looking for new ways of thinking and living—a new lifestyle. The other pressure, no less strong, was the pious movement of the scribes and Pharisees to preserve Judaism, its law, customs and traditions, by total separation from the heathen world and its influences.

When studying the manners and customs of those who lived before us, especially cultures of another place, we must be aware that a lack of understanding could easily render us blind and make even the most ancient and long-lived manners and customs appear foolish and often absurd. We should work for understanding and be slow in making judgments. ∎

The firstborn was the object of much affection and special attention, as it was customary that the firstborn male inherit certain rights and privileges. Like his father, he inherited authority over those of the family who were younger, and upon the death of the elder he received a double portion of his father's estate, and he in turn became the elder—the family head.

The choice of a bride for a son was usually made by his father. The whole family was of course interested in the selection, as the bride became a member of the immediate household.

When giving a blessing before a meal, whether spoken in Aramaic (the language of Jesus' time), old Hebrew, or even Greek, the words were well known and used by all: "Blessed art thou, Jehovah our God, King of the world, who causes to come forth bread from the earth."

As supreme ruler over his family, the elder (usually the father) had unquestioned power and authority, and was at liberty to resort to any measure, within the law, to inflict any punishment or provide any reward.

Salting the newborn baby had been a custom for centuries. The body was rubbed with salt and olive oil to tighten and firm the skin, as this was believed to insure the development of a strong healthy child.

Naming the child

Jewish tradition always considered a person's name very significant; it was not just a label, but an essential part of that person. In the first century, names were often selected from those of beloved ancestors or biblical heroes. Another custom practiced, to remind one of his ancestry, was the addition of the father's name after the son's given name—for example, Simon Bar-jonah, meaning "Simon, son of Jonah."

Often, Jews had a second name such as "Thomas which is called Didymus"—Thomas being Aramaic, the language of the day, and Didymus being Greek, but both sharing the same meaning. As a token of honor, men of rank often changed the names of those in their charge when they entered upon a new service.

Jesus' name in Aramaic was *Yeshua,* which is what he would have been called. It was a common name in his time. The name Jesus comes to us from *Iesus,* Greek for *Yeshua.*

Jewish girls were often given names taken from examples of the world around them, such as flowers or animals, or occasionally from some special characteristic of the moment of their birth.

The rite of circumcision was a covenant with God, and the act signified that the Jewish male was taken into the covenant community of God. The delicate operation of cutting away the foreskin of the infant male child was performed on the eighth day of his life, often by a specialist from outside the family. Any male, child or adult, who was uncircumcised was considered a heathen by those of the Jewish community.

A wedding procession passes to the house of the bridegroom, the way lit by oil lamps. Shortly after the marriage ceremony, the bridegroom and his friends will escort the bride to her new home and the wedding feast. Joining the bride in the procession are other virgins of her own age, each carrying a lamp and supply of oil. Friends in the procession sing and dance as they proceed through the narrow dark streets. It was the duty of the bridegroom, with the help of his family, to make all the preparations for the celebration, likely the most important one of his life.

A salutation was the means for greeting another person. Often, exaggerated gestures and expressions were used to show varying deprees of respect, or for a warm exchange of compliments with a friend. The custom of addressing as "Rabbi" those chosen to be honored was common in Jesus' time.

When receiving guests, the washing of their feet was the first act in expressing one's hospitality. This was necessary and practical as the feet became dirty when wearing only sandals. Footgear were always taken off before crossing the threshold of the house.

Another way of honoring a guest was to serve him the best morsel the host could provide. The sop, a piece of bread used to scoop up the morsel, was placed directly into the mouth of the one being honored.

Bearing gifts *when visiting persons of great influence or high rank had been the custom for centuries. Even when visiting those of equal rank or social status, gifts worthy of their station were usually given.*

The waving of palm branches was the custom at fall festivals. The palm tree, a remarkable tree, grew almost everywhere in Palestine. When carried and waved, as when the crowds met Jesus, the branches were used as a sign to honor one favored among the people.

To strike another person with the open hand expressed one's utmost contempt. This was as great an insult as one could express to another.

Sunset to sunset was considered the period of one day. In Jewish Palestine the new day always began with the setting of the sun.

Anointing the sick with oil was one of many prescriptions used to deal with physical complaints. Its softening, soothing properties, and natural healing power made oil mixed with spices or wine a highly esteemed remedy.

When reading the Scriptures aloud, it was customary to utter the words with a tone close to song—often accompanied by a swinging of the upper body.

Ashes were often sprinkled upon the head when one wanted to make an outward sign for some special act of devotion or when one was fasting. Ashes were also used to express one's deep sorrow at the death of someone dear.

The first fruits of every crop were given back to God as an expression of appreciation for the bounty received from the harvest. Only the choicest portions, the best of the firstfruits, were offered. These offerings were given to the maintenance of God's priests.

To tithe is to give to God one-tenth of all one receives as an acknowledgement that everything comes from God and belongs to God. This portion was to be given willingly and was used to support God's house, the temple.

A tenth portion of fruit and grain was determined by measure. Animals were passed under a marking rod that had been dipped in dye, and every tenth animal was designated by a mark on its back as one to be gathered and presented to God for His service.

A vow was a promise to Almighty God, voluntarily undertaken, and uttered aloud, by an individual. Vows were frequently made on recovery from sickness, or deliverance from danger or disaster, or to obtain God's mercy and favor. A vow was a solemn promise to consecrate something, such as money, property, a gift, or even a child, to God, or to do something in His service or to His honor. Without the vow, one might feel no obligation to fulfill the promise later.

Anointing the head of a guest was an ancient custom still practiced in Jesus' time. A small amount of olive oil mixed with spices was poured over the head as an expression of hospitality.

The custom of washing the hands *before eating was a ceremony usually accompanied by prayer. Upon completion of the meal, the hands were cleansed again in the same fashion. The use of the fingers for eating made this a necessary custom.*

The fatted calf or lamb *was an animal selected to provide the meat for an upcoming festive occasion, or held in reserve for honoring a special guest. In the early summer this lamb or calf would literally be hand-stuffed with food each day by the women of the house. Because of the continual stuffing, the animal gained an abnormal amount of weight.*

THE CUSTOMS OF THE DAY

On the shoulders of bearers the funeral bier was quickly moved to the tomb for interment. Only hours before, a sorrowful wail had announced to all that a death had occurred. From that moment family, friends, and neighbors of the deceased demonstrated their sorrow through weeping, tearing their garments, beating their breasts, or wearing sackcloth mourning garments. Because the burial almost always took place the same day, few preparations could be made except possibly the hiring of professional mourners to accompany the bier to the tomb.

Intense mourning would last for three to seven days as the family continued to express their grief, often at the tomb itself. Mourning, although less intense, continued for as long as a year after.

Burial took place in tombs and sepulchres, or in natural caves. For those who couldn't afford even a cave site, a simple grave would be used. Tombs and sepulchres were hand-hewn out of the soft limestone hillsides that abound in Palestine. Most tombs had more than one chamber, with the forecourt serving as a vestibule for relatives to mourn. As the tomb cross section shows, the other room(s) were burial chambers with small plat-forms, like extended fingers, carved into the walls for laying the bodies. The door to such a burial chamber was a removable stone slab. A large round stone disc that could be rolled into place was used to seal the tomb entrance.

After the flesh had decomposed, the bones left in the tomb were placed inside a limestone casket called an ossuary, thereby making room for other buri-als.

Large monumental tombs and sepulchres of the wealthy could be seen out-side Jerusalem. In the Kidron Valley stand the tombs of Zachariah (top right) and Bene-Hezir (top left), tombs surely seen by Jesus.

Preparing the Dead

Immediately upon death, family, friends, or neigh-bors prepared the body for burial. The eyes were closed, the entire body was washed and anointed with oil, and the hands and feet were then wrapped in linen bands. The body, clothed in a favorite garment, was then wrapped around with winding sheets. Spices of myrrh and aloes were placed in the folds of the garment to perfume the body. A napkin was then bound about the head, and the body was laid out for viewing in an upper room.

CHAPTER · TWELVE

MERCHANTS, TRADERS, AND PEDDLERS

The period discussed in this book was a time of growing contact between East and West, Jew and Gentile. By this time, the Jews had been living in the midst of a commercial Greek world since the Hellenization of the Bible lands by Alexander the Great. Then the Romans came and expanded upon this base by establishing additional trade between Rome and its provinces. The whole of the Mediterranean became one great marketplace.

Through these years, more Jews were living in the Greek coastal towns. It was from the Greek merchants, as years earlier from the Phoenicians, that these Jews learned much of the art of commerce, especially in international trade. They soon became serious competition for their teachers. Trade in Palestine, as everywhere, was controlled by a relative few and was very lucrative.

For the average person living in Palestine, commerce meant buying and selling in the local marketplace without much thought about how the goods got there. New goods, especially those manufactured elsewhere, were brought by ambitious merchants on the backs of heavily laden donkeys and camels. These businessmen were basically peddlers who serviced hundreds of towns and villages. They brought the outside world to the doorstep of Palestine, and the new, expensive and tempting luxury items they brought were formidable rivals to the goods already traded in the land.

With expanded development of agriculture, districts such as Galilee began to produce commodities in excess of their local needs. When these needs were met, the surplus could be exported and, with the development of outside markets, revenues would increase.

There have always been great highways crisscrossing Palestine. Some, paved with stone, remain from earlier times. Even with the additional paved roads built by the Romans, however, it was not easy to travel about Palestine, especially in rural areas where the route was often little more than a footpath. Rough dirt paths were difficult to negotiate in the best of times, and in wet weather were almost impossible. Except for paved Roman roads, most of the roads were not suited for large-wheeled vehicles, especially roads in the hill country of Judea.

Roman roads were built to last, and they did. Surfaced with cut stones fitted over a complex bed up to a meter deep, some of these roads still remain visible today. The roads, or "ways" as they were known, were marked by milestones and, in some places, curb stones and drainage ditches. These marvels of construction were built to link the various parts of the empire, both for trade and for security.

During the first century, traveling about Palestine could be extremely dangerous. In spite of Rome's efforts to rid regions of lawlessness, desolate areas provided many spots where bandits could lie in wait. They attacked unsuspecting pilgrims and traders whose precious goods were packed high on animals, and then retired to hide in the hills and caves nearby. Travel in those days was not only dangerous, but uncomfortable, and was undertaken only when absolutely essential, and never alone.

Travel by sea was limited to merchant vessels along established trade routes. Sailing along the coast between Alexandria and Rome, the grain ships were the principal means of traveling to and from Palestine by sea. Sailors could be assured of good sailing weather only between May and September, and thus avoided the sea between November and March. Spring and fall were also risky times for sea travel for both men and goods.

Even after coins of established value were minted, payment for goods could be made with equal value in other goods, or in a given weight of precious metal. It was the common practice to weigh metal coins to insure their proper value. The merchants' scales guaranteed coins that had not been clipped or filed. Inspection of the soundness of currency was, of course, crucial to trade, and was one of the important services provided by bankers and money-changers.

Other functions of bankers included arranging foreign exchange, and providing a savings system where interest could be earned on deposits. In the first century an average of 8% interest was paid on savings, and the account could be drawn upon at any time. Rich and poor alike entrusted their savings to one Jewish banker or another. Personal and business loans were a major part of the banking business. The Scriptures did not allow charging interest to a fellow Jew, but interest charged by Jewish bankers to non-Jews was high enough to make up for the loss. It is highly unlikely that this rule was always followed. Bankers would form trading associations for financing large commercial transactions, both inside Palestine and internationally.

The religious laws of the Jews strictly regulated commercial transactions involving use of weights and measures. To begin with, only approved weights could be used, although there were those who would try to substitute homemade weights or measures. Regulations did exist which specified how these important devices were to be kept honest and clean. The only legal weights that could be used were those certified true and stamped with the name of the inspector who passed them as being of accurate weight. These regulations were necessary, for weights, scales and measures were the very basis for most of the commercial transactions of the times.

The slave trade was good business and taken for granted almost universally. Slaves were considered property: commodities to be bought and sold at will. Not only were the slaves themselves owned, but items in their possession belonged to their owners. Strict regulations controlled the owning of Jewish slaves, especially a Jewess. For example, Jewish law forbade one Jew to buy another Jew as a slave. But this does not mean there were no Jewish slaves of Jews.

Those owning Jewish slaves knew their slaves were not required to serve more than seven years, as all slaves were released on the year of Jubilee, the seventh year in the cycle. This meant that slaves sold in the fifth year of a cycle were not as valuable as slaves sold in the first year, who had six years yet to serve.

In the East, Tyre was the center of the Gentile slave trade, with both male and female slaves coming through that important market. It should be remembered that half of the sixty million or so people who lived under the Eagle of Rome were slaves. In spite of this, slavery played no significant part in the lives of those living in Palestine, especially in rural areas. Only in the urban centers could slaves be found, usually working there as domestic servants.

The Jews of Palestine learned the art of commerce quickly and very well. By the first century many Jews had become successful traders and international merchants, changing forever the interaction of Palestine with the outside world.

■

Bargaining always provided the haggler an enjoyable and exciting experience, whether he was selling his standing crop, purchasing something expensive and extravagant, or simply buying daily necessities. Both parties would shout with excitement, the seller always asking twice the price he expected and the buyer offering only half of what he intended to pay. Soon a price was established, with both the buyer and seller convinced they got the best of the deal.

MERCHANTS, TRADERS, AND PEDDLERS

The banker was entrusted with the safekeeping of the capital of the rich and poor alike, and for this he was paid a handsome interest rate. He would take these funds and lend them for commercial transactions at a considerably higher rate than he paid his savings clients. Although the law of Moses forbids loans with interest to other Jews, the Jewish bankers could, and did, charge high rates to the Gentile. An exorbitant interest rate, in the 20%–30% range, was charged by all bankers, Jew and Gentile alike.

A nomad trader leads his camel to a nearby local market. His goods would consist of a mix of items for which he traded elsewhere in the desert. It was in the villages on the fringe of the desert that he hoped to sell his exotic goods.

The art and science of the Jewish people, both theoretical and applied, developed over the centuries under influences from the many sophisticated cultures with which they had come in contact.

Applied engineering was everywhere in the form of mechanical devices including pulleys, levers, and locks. Casting, in metal and clay, was highly developed. Medicine, physics, and geometry were well known. Mathematics and astronomy were used for computing the lunar calendar. Agricultural and horticultural knowledge were advancing.

Jewish art was significant in that it excluded the representation of men, women or animals because it was prohibited by the Torah. Art consisted solely of the representation of plants and geometric designs. Shown above are examples of these designs and a stone hemicycle, a form of sundial. The time is indicated where the shadow of the pointer intersects the inscribed lines.

Paper, Pen, and Ink

Writing in first-century Palestine was done in Aramaic, Greek and ancient Hebrew. Aramaic was the everyday language of the Jews, as Greek was of the Gentiles. Ancient Hebrew was read in the temple and synagogue and written only to make copies of the Old Testament text. Few could read or write the alphabet of their forefathers. (Hebrew and Aramaic are written and read from right to left, from top line to bottom of the column, while Greek is written left to right.)

Text was often written in narrow columns approximately two to three inches wide on specially prepared leather, papyrus, or parchment. A scroll was made from sheets sewn together to form a roll; these varied in length—some up to forty feet. One side was unrolled while the other was rolled so that a long scroll could be managed.

Ink was usually black and made from soot with a gum or oil binder. Red ink was also available. It was made from iron oxides pressed into cakes that required moistening before application. Black ink was kept in a small clay or bronze inkwell. The reed pen was carved in a fashion similar to the quill pen.

Wax tablets, often with a hinged protective cover, were used for short temporary notes or messages. They were never used for permanent records. The words were scratched onto the wax with a sharp pointed stylus (its opposite end was flat for rubbing out mistakes). After each use the wax was smoothed and used again.

Potsherds, or ostraca, were pieces of broken pottery, handy for scratched notes and receipts to be discarded after use.

Private letters could be folded or rolled and sealed with wax to ensure private use. To seal a papyrus or parchment document, it was first folded into a narrow strip, further folded into thirds, and then tied with a string and sealed with wax.

Scrolls were rolled and stored in racks or pottery jars with airtight lids.

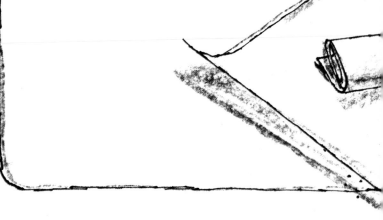

Most travelers on "the way" *were traders and merchants going from village to village. With their tempting wares piled high upon their donkeys, they would plan their route to arrive in the larger towns in time for the feasts and local fairs.*

When "the way" was wet and slippery, most travelers took off their sandals for better footing. This also conserved their valuable sandals from the abuse they would receive on the primitive roadways.

For a long journey the donkey was the mount to use. It had no equal for keeping a solid footing on the stony and often muddy roadways, it could carry a substantial load, and it could maintain an even pace no matter what the terrain.

When nighttime overtook a traveler far from a village or inn, it usually meant sleeping by the roadside. He would simply find a stone for a pillow and wrap his mantle around his body for warmth, probably lamenting his ill fortune.

Wheeled vehicles were not unknown in Palestine, but they had only limited use. The rough hilly country proved unsuitable for large, wheeled vehicles, so they were used mainly on the level coastal plains. They were used much more extensively on the paved Roman roads. Wagons were used in the massive building projects of Herod, when he had some four hundred heavy-duty wagons built to haul materials for the temple construction.

The ox-drawn cart with the lattice box was used for commercial hauling, and probably for short trips only. The covered wagon would have been horse-drawn and used by the army for hauling baggage and supplies. It probably carried mail and passengers over the paved Roman roads as well. The small wooden cart would have had extensive service for the faster transport of vital commercial goods such as foodstuffs, and possibly for an occasional passenger.

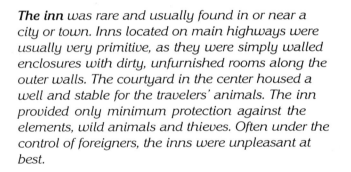

The inn was rare and usually found in or near a city or town. Inns located on main highways were usually very primitive, as they were simply walled enclosures with dirty, unfurnished rooms along the outer walls. The courtyard in the center housed a well and stable for the travelers' animals. The inn provided only minimum protection against the elements, wild animals and thieves. Often under the control of foreigners, the inns were unpleasant at best.

The clay amphora was a sturdy commercial container that held perishables or liquids. Merchants could tell at a glance the quantity and contents of these vessels made in standard sizes and shapes. Though large enough to hold a large quantity (the middle-sized vessel shown holds approximately six gallons), it was small enough to be handled by one man and could be carried by the handles or rolled on the spindle-like base. The pointed base also provided a helpful handle when lifting or pouring.

The camel was an exceptional beast of burden, the long-distance freight vehicle of the day. Despite its forbidding appearance and volatile temperament, the camel was a delicate beast. It required proper attention and care as its service was absolutely essential for long-distance travel. Enabled to retain both food and water, it could go for days without either. When it could eat, its staple food was grass, bushes and wild flowers. Its droppings were used as fuel and the female camel's milk was used as food, both important for travel in the wilderness.

Pack and riding saddles were made of leather sacking, stuffed with padding attached to a wooden frame. The saddle cover was made of sheepskin with additional cushions and horns. Saddle bags were often hung at the sides.

Roman roads *were a lifeline between the principal trade centers and capitals throughout the empire. Built not only to aid commerce, but to facilitate troop movements and speed courier service, the roads provided an important link in communication and security.*

The roads were under the army's jurisdiction. Part of the duty of the army was not only to build these roads, but to keep them in good repair. Rock and dirt slides washing onto the roadbed demanded constant attention.

Many of the great ancient trade routes passed through Palestine, which lay at the strategic point where Europe, Asia, and Africa meet. Merchants with their heavy-laden camel caravans from many lands could be seen regularly traversing these historical routes.

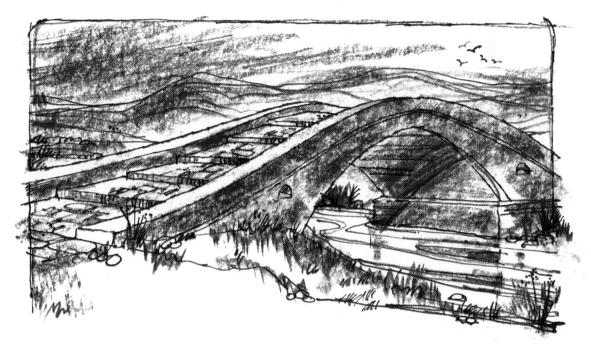

The only bridge over the Jordan River was built by the Romans and was called "the bridge of the sons of Jacob."

Roman merchant ships sailed the Mediterranean Sea with grain, cargo, and passengers, and linked land caravans and travelers with the vast empire. Although cumbersome, because of their poor maneuverability, these ships were reasonably fast.

Most Jewish merchants did not own merchant ships but hired Greek, Phoenician and Roman vessels to handle their shipments. Travelers made their way from port to port on these vessels. Reasonably comfortable, the ships provided scheduled passenger service throughout the Mediterranean. Caesarea and Joppa were the major ports from which one could enter or leave Palestine during the first century.

Exports and Imports

Between the provinces of the empire, goods went both by ship and caravan. From Palestine, exports consisted almost entirely of agricultural products, including wine, wheat, olive oil, balsam, honey, and figs.

Imports, such as these illustrated, were chiefly luxury goods, including precious metals to be used for jewelry and coins. For the wealthy consumer, fashionable sandals, fabrics, glass and metal lamps, or a Hellenistic vase were imported.

Liquid commodities were exported in commercial amphoras, that were themselves imported to Palestine.

Slavery was taken for granted in the first century. The number of slaves in Palestine was not significant and played no great part outside the urban centers. In wealthy homes, slaves worked mostly as domestic servants.

There were at least three ways by which a Jew might become a slave. Sometimes a person would sell himself into service because of debt or extreme poverty. In other instances a person might become a slave in order to make restitution as a convicted thief. A less common event was when a father sold his young daughter into domestic service to another Jew. The intent was that she would marry into the family when she came of age. On her twelfth birthday she returned to her father's home if a marriage had not taken place, as no Jew could own an adult Jewess.

The Romans, on the other hand, were often cruel to, and usually very demanding of, their many slaves. Even the Roman ladies were notorious for barbarous treatment of their handmaidens. Young black female slaves were common and highly preferred as domestics in Roman homes throughout the empire.

Slaves who offended or were caught stealing were scourged. Jewish owners often badly treated foreign slaves, whereas their Jewish slaves were often regarded as part of the family.

The religious law of the Jews strictly regulated all commercial transactions involving the use of weights and measures. Scales were to be kept clean and only true weights were to be used.

Coins were minted in Palestine in much the same manner as elsewhere in the ancient world. Molten metal was poured into stone molds with blank coin slots. These metal blanks were then removed from the molds and inserted between dies engraved with the desired images, one die for each side. A hammer blow would imprint the images into the soft metal. Each coin was then weighed and excess precious metal was trimmed or filed off, care being taken that each coin's weight was identical. The coin was then polished before entering circulation.

Palm

Span

Measurements

With this system, one always had with him the means of making measurements, although there were differences because each person varied in size. The smallest unit was the "finger," with the "palm" or "handbreath" next in size. The "span" was an easy measurement to make. The "cubit" was an important measurement that varied between five and seven handbreaths. According to some scholars the medium cubit ranged between 40.6 cm. to 66 cm. The commonly accepted unit was 43.7 cm., the unit used in the construction of Herod's Temple and in commerce as well.

Finger

1 Cubit

CHAPTER·THIRTEEN

THE OCCUPIED AND OCCUPIER

When thinking of Jesus' world, a fundamental fact to keep in mind is that Palestine was an occupied land, a very small part of a vast empire that extended from Asia, around the entire Mediterranean Sea to the distant Atlantic Ocean in the west.

Foreign occupation was not new to this land. Over the centuries the Jewish kingdoms of Israel and Judea had been overrun by a succession of powerful nations, each making every effort to impose foreign ideals upon its Jewish subjects. Rome was no exception. No matter how remote, Rome's presence was seen and felt every day, as it administered the empire through direct control, or, in outlying areas, through loyal servants.

Shortly before the first century, the Roman empire was divided into senatorial and imperial provinces, with most falling into the senatorial class under the control of the Roman Senate. The few provinces that fell into the imperial class were those most difficult to govern, thus requiring a strong military presence. These came under the direct control of the emperor himself. Among them was the province of Syria, with tiny Palestine under its jurisdiction.

Syria was governed by a Roman official of senatorial rank, whose support and authority came directly from the emperor. What impact did this governor's immense power have upon the day-to-day daily and religious life of the Jew in Palestine? First, let us look at when and how Palestine came under the shadow of the Eagle of Rome.

The Eagle crossed the sea in 63 B.C. with Pompey and his vast army, and swept across Palestine. Once in Jerusalem, Jewish independence came to an abrupt end. Palestine proper was soon annexed to the larger province of Syria. With the blessing of Rome, Herod was established as King of the Jews and ruled both Jew and Gentile with absolute authority. The only check to his oppression and cruelty was concern over how Rome might interpret his actions. Just four short years before the first century A.D., Herod the Great died.

The Kingdom of Herod was divided between his three sons: Philip, Archelaus, and Herod Antipas. Antipas was the best-known son and, as tetrarch, was to rule the territory of upper and lower Galilee, and a second, unconnected part to the east known as Peraea. It was this new ruler who imprisoned and later executed John the Baptist as one of his more infamous acts. Jesus implied He knew Herod's cruel and cunning ways when He called Herod a fox.

Philip was to rule territories northeast of Galilee, outside Palestine proper. Unlike his father, he was an honorable man and ruled his predominantly Greek population with justice. It was a peaceful reign that ended in A.D. 34 with Philip's death.

Archelaus received the prize: Judea and its great city, Jerusalem; Samaria and the port city of Caesarea; and, in the south, Idumea, the homeland of his father. Even with the promise of more power if he succeeded, Archelaus misgoverned. His oppressive and bloody rule earned him the worst possible reputation in Rome. He was soon summoned to account for himself, deposed and banished to an outpost in Gaul. The territory of Judea, as it was known in Rome, was immediately put under the direct control of the empire under the governship of a procurator. Because of this drastic change, the people of Judea were to experience direct Roman control unlike anything they had known to date.

In Judea the Romans adopted their

standard provincial policy of subjugation by intimidation, a policy that could not have been more incompatible with Jewish religions and philosophy. At least Herod and his sons had understood the Jews and Judaism. But the new Roman governor had no such understanding or appreciation, and he soon found himself in much difficulty and frustration because of this lack of understanding.

Most governors could see the Jewish religion and traditions only as instruments to achieve the goals of Rome. Thus the relationship between the Jewish population and the governing procurators soon became strained and ultimately hostile.

Although the Romans abused their power, occasionally they could be considerate of their subjects, and, as in the case of the Jews, make allowances to accommodate their religious ideals. For example, worship of the emperor was not demanded, nor was military service required. The Jews responded to their favored position by initiating a daily offering in the temple for Caesar and the Roman people. Roman coins and the standards of the army, with their images of gods and the emperor, were a problem, but one treated with tolerance. By their own rule, troops were not allowed to bring image-bearing standards within the walls of the holy city of Jerusalem, and coins could easily be exchanged for "clean" coins by a money-changer in the court of the temple. Having one's name on a Roman census list was also a problem, as there was something offensive and threatening about being counted and listed.

Rome itself gave other major concessions to this small province. First, the government permitted Jerusalem to remain as the capital of the Jewish community and its temple as the religious center. The temple was permitted to function, as before, with its daily worship and observance of festivals. The teaching of the law could be practiced, as before, in synagogues throughout Palestine.

The Jewish leadership was also recognized and was given, within limits, the power to exercise its own laws. The administration of this civil and religious law was in the hands of the Jewish supreme court—the Sanhedrin. It was an aristocratic institution dominated by the temple priesthood. The Sanhedrin was a powerful force in first-century Jewish life.

In the benevolent Jewish courts, the hope was always that if an error in judgment occurred, that error would favor the accused; but, if a judgment were made against him, his punishment would be administered immediately after the trial and in the presence of the judge and the witnesses against the accused. Crucifixion was not a punishment of the Jewish court, but an ancient form of execution adopted by the Romans. For an unspeakable crime, crucifixion was an effective punishment, especially when a painful, lingering death was desired. In Bible lands this kind of execution became frightfully common.

Execution by crucifixion began immediately after conviction and sentencing was pronounced. Flogging usually preceded the procession to the outskirts of the city. A route was chosen that would attract as much attention as possible, for the crowd would often follow to witness the execution. A white wooden board with the nature of the crime printed upon it was carried in front of the procession, later to be attached above the victim's head. Once at the site outside the city wall, the soldiers began the gruesome procedure of nailing the victim to the cross on which he was to be suspended. The lingering agony continued until his death. The detachment stood guard until the body was taken down and removed for burial.

Rome had only one kind of army, a permanent professional organization. Its officers and troops existed for two major reasons: to keep the peace and to protect the empire by whatever means required.

The military organization in the East could be separated into three distinct groups. The first was the legion itself, a well-trained, well-equipped war-machine, that was stationed in Syria, primarily to guard the Parthian frontier. The second were the legion support units—the auxiliary. These troops were the archers, slingers and cavalry who had been recruited locally in the eastern provinces. The third was a special group of 3,000 soldiers stationed in Judea as a garrison. The garrison was used to keep order, to fight minor skirmishes, and especially to perform daily police duties. These lightly armed mercenaries, inherited from Herod and commanded by regular legion officers, were considered inferior in every way to legion troops or its auxiliary.

In general, the legion was made up of volunteers from the western provinces. The majority of these men were rough peasants bearing little similarity to those in the stately Praetorian guard stationed in Rome. The legionaries were mostly farm boys, especially well-suited for the long days of hard physical labor, forced marches and harsh battles that the empire required of its homesick sons stationed on a frontier. This well-disciplined force maintained the flexibility necessary to operate either as an autonomous unit or in harmony with other legions.

The armies of the empire conquered many lands, and wherever they conquered they established miniature versions of Rome. This was true of Palestine and Syria where the works of the soldier/builder could be seen everywhere. Broad paved highways, public baths, and theaters abounded, especially in the hellenized towns and cities. The outlying frontier also gained benefits because of the Roman presence, since the Romans established new markets, bought raw materials, and promoted their Graeco-Roman culture.

The military presence also served as a constant reminder of the authority of Rome as the troops maintained the elaborate defense system necessary to protect cultural, military and political gains. This system included a string of fortresses and strongholds at strategic points which were maintained primarily by local garrisons.

The importation of the Hellenistic culture into Palestine had a strong influence on the people and soon developed into an acceptable way of life. Wealthy Jews were attracted to its commerce and materialism. Greek soon became the accepted language for trade and commerce, and profits could be gained by accepting the new language and its cultural values. Even the less affluent who lived in or near hellenized Greek cities and towns found themselves obligated, whether for convenience, or survival, to learn the Greek language and Greek ways. This interaction with the pagan was so intense that within a few short years many lost the use of the Aramaic language.

Jewish religious leaders' concern over this infiltration was real. How could they adequately defend against contamination by the pagans and their lifestyle? Many Jews indulged themselves in the foreign culture, for its houses, goods and clothing had great appeal. Herod and his sons vigorously promoted the

culture of the Romans and many others accepted its appealing way of life, even though it was a lifestyle wholly incompatible with Jewish culture and religion.

There was, at the same time, however, great resistance by most Jews to this direct influence, both in Jerusalem and throughout Palestine. It was the final misfortune of these reluctant to change that they disregarded the effect of this Graeco-Roman culture on their lives and underestimated the immense power of the Roman empire. ∎

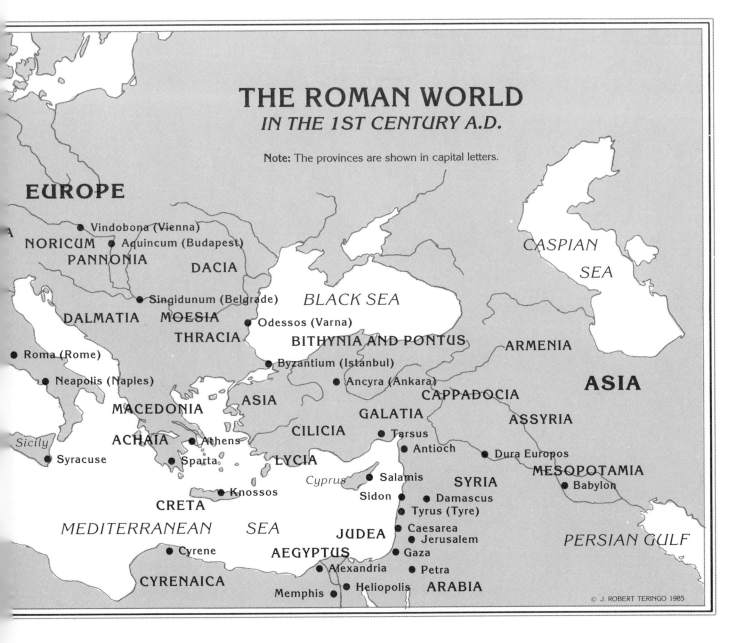

THE ROMAN WORLD
IN THE 1ST CENTURY A.D.

Note: The provinces are shown in capital letters.

EUROPE

NORICUM • Vindobona (Vienna)
• Aquincum (Budapest)
PANNONIA
DACIA

Singidunum (Belgrade) • BLACK SEA
DALMATIA MOESIA
• Odessos (Varna)
THRACIA BITHYNIA AND PONTUS

CASPIAN SEA

ARMENIA

• Roma (Rome)
• Byzantium (Istanbul)
• Neapolis (Naples) • Ancyra (Ankara)
ASIA
MACEDONIA ASIA CAPPADOCIA
GALATIA ASSYRIA
ACHAIA CILICIA • Tarsus
Sicily • Athens LYCIA • Antioch • Dura Europos
• Syracuse • Sparta Cyprus • Salamis MESOPOTAMIA
• Knossos Sidon SYRIA • Babylon
CRETA • Damascus
• Tyrus (Tyre)
MEDITERRANEAN SEA JUDEA • Caesarea PERSIAN GULF
• Cyrene AEGYPTUS • Jerusalem
• Gaza
• Alexandria • Petra
CYRENAICA • Heliopolis ARABIA
Memphis •

© J. ROBERT TERINGO 1985

0 KILOMETERS 500
0 STATUTE MILES 300

The procurator was the Roman governor of Judea. The first governor was appointed in A.D. 6, after the territories of Herod's son Archelaus were placed under the direct control of Rome. The procurator had complete authority in the internal affairs of Judea. His chief concerns were with justice and finance; he kept the peace and collected the taxes. The best-remembered procurator was Pontius Pilate (A.D. 26–36), who offended the Jews on many occasions and also sanctioned the execution of Jesus. He was finally replaced some years after that event, charged with "endless and intolerable crimes."

Spiritual authority was placed by Rome in the hands of a council of high priests. From the time of Herod the Great to the destruction of Jerusalem, twenty-eight different high priests exercised complete spiritual authority over the Jewish people.

The religion and nationality of the Jews in Palestine were recognized by Rome. Although the province was occupied, it was Rome's usual policy to allow its subjects to continue under their own administration, often through Roman-controlled officials, however.

The Sanhedrin and Jewish Justice

The administration of the civil and religious law in Palestine was in the hands of Jewish courts, who made decisions according to Jewish law. The Sanhedrin, although limited by Roman authority, possessed power to try, convict, and carry out sentences, with one exception—the execution of the death sentence required confirmation by the Roman governor.

The Sanhedrin was a council of seventy elders, with the high priest presiding over the priestly aristocrats and dominating its proceedings. It did, however, administer justice with remarkable impartiality and benevolence.

Every town of any size had a tribunal to deal with local matters of law and religion.

The taxes from Judea, as an imperial province, went into the treasury of the emperor, meaning that taxes were paid directly to Caesar.

Taxes were always collected by Roman officials, who were backed by Roman might. Custom taxes, or indirect taxes, were farmed out to tax collectors, or publicans, who leased districts from the Romans for a fixed sum. Abundant room for interpretation of rates left the tax collector in a position to take advantage and overcharge. Whatever he collected in excess of the prescribed rate was his gain. This exploitation made the tax collectors a class hated by the population. On the other hand, many of these same people were very inventive in ways to defraud the tax collector.

The tax obligation of the Romans consisted of a land tax and a poll tax levied on every male child over fourteen years, and every female over twenty years; only the aged were exempt. There were other taxes or duties on imports and exports. Local tolls, dues and market fees added to the burden.

The slinger belonged to an auxiliary unit attached to the regular army legion. An accomplished slinger could hurl missiles from his leather sling with great force and range, sending his stone, clay or lead missile in excess of one hundred meters.

The auxiliary archer used his arrows for assault at a distance. His short sword was for hand-to-hand combat. He carried many arrows, some of which were firebrands, used for setting fires at great distances. His composite bow was made of wood with tips of bone or horn, and the string was made from the sinew of an animal.

The Auxiliary and His Gear

The equipment of the legion auxiliary differed from that of the legionary in two respects. First, the weapons and protective gear of the auxiliary were lighter, and second, most of his equipment was inferior to that of the regular army. Each group of eight auxiliary soldiers was allocated camp equipment, including a tent and cooking gear, as well as a donkey with which to transport it.

The garrison of infantry and cavalry stationed in Judea was formed from the old troops of Herod the Great for use by the procurator as a peace-time police and guard force. These troops were under the direct control of the procurator and comprised approximately three thousand men. Most of these were stationed in Caesarea, with the exception of one cohort in Jerusalem and small detachments at fortresses across Judea.

The main force was made up of local mercenaries from the cities of Caesarea and Sebaste. The "Sebastenes," as they were known, were divided into five cohorts of infantry, with five hundred soldiers to each cohort, and centurions from regular legions in command.

The cavalry, of five hundred troopers and horses, was necessary for riot control, pursuit or swift assaults. The speed and agility of horses allowed for a quick response to any given situation, often before the enemy could react.

The legionary was the basic foot soldier of the Roman army. He was the world's best-trained and disciplined soldier, well-equipped to do his job, whether in a small skirmish or in a major assault.

The life of the soldier was rough and rugged, even for those un-schooled farmboys, and filled with daily drills, manual labor, forced marches and guard duty, not to say anything of the horrible battles he would face. His dreams were of his discharge, when he would be given a grant of land, usually on the frontier where he had served, to marry and farm again.

The standard embodied the spirit of the empire, and often included images of its gods and the emperor. For these reasons, standards were revered. To lose a standard in battle was the greatest disgrace.

It was from the hornblower that the soldiers received their orders, whether in camp or in the midst of battle. No action was ever taken without first receiving a signal from the Cornicen.

The tribune was a semi-professional officer who generally held his military post as a step in a political career. He was known by the purple stripe on his tunic. A tribune was appointed from an upper-middle-class family and was employed as a staff officer at headquarters. In times of crisis, or on a campaign, he often found himself in command of a front-line detachment or cohort.

The centurion was the backbone of the regular army, as well as the Roman link to the auxiliary forces. He commanded one hundred fighting men who were ready to die at his command. He was the active day-to-day officer who drilled, supervised and regulated the conduct of the common soldiers in his command.

He was required to be a tough, professional soldier who could be brutal when required, yet exemplify reasonable character. A good centurion could be all this, but was not above taking bribes from those who wished to avoid some distasteful duty. In the twenty-five years of his enlistment, he hoped to rise through the ranks and become senior in his cohort, the best of five centurions.

Siege equipment was used to neutralize a fortified position. Before an assault, catapults of different sizes were used to wreak havoc and drive the defenders from their positions.

A small, portable crossbow called the "scorpion" was used to instill fear in the hearts of defenders. It silently shot large, iron-tipped arrows great distances. The larger, stonethrowing catapult hurled stones through the walls of buildings hundreds of feet away.

Under the cover of the catapult barrage, platforms and towers would be moved into position against the walls. A tower supported a swinging battering ram as well as a platform for assault troops. While the ram battered away at the wall, slingers and archers on top would pelt the exposed defenders on the ramparts.

The Equipment of the Legionary

The defense and attack equipment of the Roman soldier was carefully designed and manufactured. For defense each legionary carried a large curved shield (A), curved so as to protect the body better. Made of thin strips of wood glued together, it was covered by leather with bronze binding around its edge. A circular center boss provided a handgrip. A bronze or leather helmet (B) protected the head and neck. In A.D. 14, a new type of body armor was introduced—articulated plate armor (C). It covered the chest, shoulders and back, while on the dagger belt (D), leather straps with metal disks (E) hung to protect the loins.

For attack the legionary carried two kinds of weapons, the short double-edged sword (F) and the pilum (javelin) (G). Each man had two pilum to be thrown at first encounter, while still at some distance from his enemy. The pilum was designed to pierce the shield of an enemy soldier and bend. Encumbered by a seven-foot pilum, it was impossible for the enemy to use his shield for defense; many made the mistake of dropping the shield entirely, thus forced to fight the Roman soldier unprotected.

To prolong the suffering the victim would be bound with ropes, or provided a sedile (seat) to reduce the pressure on his arms and chest cavity. To make the pain tolerable he was often given drugged wine as he begged to be put out of his misery.

Death came slowly as the thirst, cramps, pain, and the extreme difficulty of breathing made for the most horrible suffering one can imagine. The only way for the condemned to gain breath was to draw up the body by the legs and lessen the pressure on his arms and chest cavity. When the legs were broken it became impossible to breathe, and death by asphyxia followed the tetanic contraction (cramps) of the respiratory muscles. All who were crucified died asphyxiated. After death the extreme rigidity of the body was immediate.

Crucifixion was a barbaric punishment, described by those who have seen its horrors as "the most wretched of deaths." Used by the Romans for those who committed violent crimes, sedition or robbery, it was considered the ultimate in public humiliation and torture.

Crucifixion took many forms. There were the single post or stake; the traditional cross, posts crossed in the shape of an X; and, as illustrated, a post with a crossbeam along the top in the form of a T. Some victims were impaled upside-down or by their private parts; some hung with outstretched arms, others with raised arms; some were seated on a peg or block, others were left hanging. For the condemned, the design of the cross or his position did not matter; in each case he was destined to suffer a lingering, agonizing death.

The foreign lifestyle of the Hellenistic world
surrounded the Jews of Palestine and slowly con-
taminated their environment. Although this pagan
culture was generally regarded with contempt, being
contrary to the law of Moses, the appeal of the
culture tempted and attracted many Jews.

Some wealthy Jews adopted the Greek lifestyle
quite readily. Having a natural affection for the
pampered life in luxurious estates, the extravagance
of these Jews was well known throughout the empire.
The merchants, bankers and land owners of Jerusalem set the social scene for the province Syria.

The youth were drawn to the concept of
"perfection of mind and body" and found a haven in
exercise rooms, gymnasiums and nude athletic
contests. Many of the older Jews loved the grand
public baths and public complexes. In the theaters,
popular pantomimes, farces, and lively comedy had
strong appeal, even though they were often crude
and obscene.

These strong influences soon led to the total
acceptance of the Graeco-Roman culture by many
Jews and non-Jews of first-century Palestine.

BIBLIOGRAPHY

Adams, J. McKee. *Biblical Backgrounds*. Nashville, Tenn.: Broadman Press, 1965.

Aharoni, Yohanon & Avi-Yonah, Michael. *Bible Atlas*. New York: Macmillan Publishing Co., 1977.

Albright, William Foxwell. *The Archaeology of Palestine*. Harmondsworth-Middlesex: Penguin Books, 1949.

Avigad, Nahman. *Discovering Jerusalem*. Jerusalem: Shikmona Publishing Co., 1980.

Avi-Yonah, Michael, ed. *Encyclopedia of Archaeological Excavations in the Holy Land*, Vol. II. Jerusalem: The Israel Exploration Society, 1976.

_____. *Gazetteer of Roman Palestine*. Jerusalem: Hebrew University of Jerusalem, 1976.

_____. ed. *The World History of the Jewish People—The Herodian Period*. New Brunswick: Rutgers University Press, 1975.

Baly, Denis. *Geographical Companion to the Bible*. New York: McGraw-Hill Book Co., 1963.

Barbet, Pierre. *A Doctor at Calvary*. Garden City, N.Y.: Image Books, 1963.

Barrett, C. K. *The New Testament Background: Selected Documents*. New York: Harper & Row, 1961.

Barrows, Rev. E. P. *Sacred Geography and Antiquities*. New York: American Tract Society, 1870.

Barton, George A. *Archaeology and the Bible*. Philadelphia: American Sunday-School Union, 1916.

Bentwich, Norman. *Hellenism*. Philadelphia: The Jewish Publication Society of America, 1919.

Bissell, Edwin Cone. *Biblical Antiquities*. Philadelphia: The American Sunday-School Union, 1893.

Blaiklock, E. M. & Harrison, R. K., eds. *New International Dictionary of Biblical Archaeology*. Grand Rapids, Mich.: Regency, 1983.

Bonsirven, Joseph. *Palestinian Judaism in the Time of Jesus Christ*. New York: Holt, Rinehart and Winston, 1964.

Booth, Henry Kendall. *The World of Jesus*. New York: Charles Scribner's Sons, 1933.

Borer, Mary Cathcart. *Two Thousand Years Ago*. London: Sir Isaac Pitman & Sons, 1961.

Bouquet, A. C. *Everyday Life in New Testament Times*. London: B. T. Batsford, 1954.

Brandon, S. G. F. *Jesus and the Zealots*. New York: Charles Scribner's Sons, 1967.

Bryant T. A., compiler. *Today's Dictionary of the Bible*. Minneapolis, Bethany House Publishers, 1982.

Burrows, Millar. *The Dead Sea Scrolls*. New York: The Viking Press, 1955.

Cansdale, George. *All the Animals of the Bible Lands*. Grand Rapids, Mich.: Zondervan Publishing House, 1970.

Casson, Lionel. *The Ancient Mariners*. New York: The Macmillan Publishing Co., 1959.

_____. *Ships and Seamanship in the Ancient World*. Princeton, N.J.: Princeton University Press, 1971.

Chandler, Walter M. *The Trial of Jesus*, (2 vol.). New York: The Federal Book Co., 1925.

Cobern, Camden M. *The New Archeological Discoveries*. New York: Funk & Wagnalls Co., 1929.

Connolly, Peter. *The Roman Army*. London: MacDonald Educational, 1976.

Cornfeld, Gaalya, gen. ed. *Josephus: The Jewish War*. Grand Rapids: Zondervan Publishing House, 1982.

Daniel-Rops, Henri. *Jesus and His Times*. New York: E. P. Dutton & Co., 1957.

_____. *Daily Life in the Time of Jesus*. New York: Hawthorn Books, 1962.

Davenport, Millia. *The Book of Costume*, (2 vol.). New York: Crown Publishers, 1948.

Davies, A. Powell. *The Meaning of the Dead Sea Scrolls*. New York: Mentor Books, 1956.

Delitzsch, Franz. *Jewish Artisan Life in the Time of Jesus*. New York: Funk & Wagnalls Co., 1883.

DeQuincey, Thomas. *Toilette of the Hebrew Lady*. Hartford, Conn.: Edwin Valentine Mitchell, 1926.

A Dictionary of the Holy Bible. New York: American Tract Society, 1859.

Duckat, Walter. *Beggar to King*. New York: Doubleday & Co., 1968.

Edersheim, Alfred. *Sketches of Jewish Social Life in the Days of Christ*. Grand Rapids, Mich.: Wm. B. Eerdman's Publishing Co., 1982.

_____. *The Life and Times of Jesus the Messiah*, (2 vol.). New York: E. R. Herrick & Co., 1886.

_____. *The Temple*. New York: Hodder & Stoughton, 1908.

Entwistle, Mary. *The Bible Guide Book*. London: Student Christian Movement Press, 1936.

Everyday Life In Bible Times. Washington, D. C.: National Geographic Society, 1968.

Farmer, William Reuben. *Maccabees, Zealots, and Josephus*. New York: Columbia University Press, 1956.

Finkelstein, Louis. *The Pharisees*, (2 vol.). Philadelphia: The Jewish Publication Society of America, 1938.

Foerster, Werner. *From the Exile to Christ*. Philadelphia: Fortress Press, 1976.

_____. *Palestinian Judaism in New Testament Times*. Edinborgh and London: Oliver and Boyd, 1967.

Forder, Archibald. *Daily Life in Palestine*. London: Marshall Brothers, 1912.

Freeman, A. M. *Manners & Customs of the Bible*. New York: Nelson & Phillips, 1874.

Friedlander, Ludwig. *Roman Life and Manners Under the Early Empire*, (4 vol.). London: George Routledge & Sons.

Glueck, Nelson. *Deities and Dolphins*. New York: Farrar, Straus and Giroux, 1965.

_____. *Rivers in the Desert*. New York: Farrar, Straus and Cudahy, 1959.

_____. *The River Jordan*. Philadelphia: The Jewish Publication Society of America, 1946.

Golub, Jacob S. *In the Days of the Second Temple*. Cincinnati: Union of American Hebrew Congregations, 1929.

Grant, Elihu. *The People of Palestine*. Philadelphia & London: J. B. Lippincott Co., 1907.

Grant, Frederick C. *Roman Hellenism and the New Testament*. New York: Charles Scribner's Sons, 1962.

Grant, Michael. *Herod the Great*. New York: American Heritage Press, 1971.

Grant, Robert M. *Early Christianity & Society*. London: Collins, 1978.

Great People of the Bible and How They Lived. Pleasantville, N.Y.: The Reader's Digest Association, 1971.

Guignebert, Charles. *The Jewish World in the Time of Jesus*. New Hyde Park, N.Y.: University Books, 1959.

Halley, Henry H. *Halley's Bible Handbook*. Grand Rapids: Zondervan Publishing House, 1962.

Henderson, Rev. Archibald. *Palestine*. Edinburgh: T. & T. Clark, 1893.

Hengel, Martin. *Crucifixion*. Philadelphia: Fortress Press, 1977.

Hitchcock, Roswell D., ed. *Complete Analysis of the Holy Bible*. New York: A. J. Johnson, 1869.

Horne, Thomas Hartwell. *An Introduction to the Critical Study and Knowledge of the Holy Scriptures*, (2 vol.). Philadelphia: De Silver, Thomas & Co., 1836.

Houghton, W. *Gleanings from the Natural History of the Ancients*. London: Cassell, Petter, Galpin & Co.

Hurlbut, J. L. *The Rand-McNally Bible Atlas*. Chicago: Rand-McNally & Co., 1910.

Jahn, Johann, tr. by Thomas C. Upham. *Jahn's Biblical Archaeology*. New York: J. Leavitt, 1832.

Jeremias, Joachim. *Jerusalem in the Time of Jesus*. London: SCM Press, 1969.

Jerusalem Revealed. Jerusalem: The Israel Exploration Society, 1975.

Johnson, Mary. *Roman Life*. Chicago: Scott, Foresman and Co., 1957.

Judge, E. A. *The Social Pattern of Christian Groups in the First Century*. London: The Tyndale Press, 1960.

Judson, Harry Pratt. *Caesar's Army*. New York: Biblo and Tanner, 1888.

Keller, Werner. *The Bible As History*. New York: William Morrow and Co., 1956.

Kitto, John. *The History of Palestine*. Boston: Gould and Lincoln, 1856.

Illustrated New Testament. Collegeville, Minn.: The Liturgical Press, 1964.

Landau, Jacob M. *Abdul-Hamid's Palestine*. London: André Deutsch, 1979.

LaSor, William Sanford. *Daily Life in Bible Times*. Cincinnati: Standard Publishing, 1956.

Levine, Lee I., ed. *Ancient Synagogues Revealed*. Jerusalem: The Israel Exploration Society, 1981.

Lockyer, Herbert. *All the Trades and Occupations of the Bible*. Grand Rapids: Zondervan Publishing House, 1971.

Loffreda, Stanislao. *A Visit to Capharnaum*. Jerusalem: Franciscan Printing Press, 1976.

MacKay, Alastair I. *Farming and Gardening in the Bible*. Emmaus, Penn.: Rodale Press, 1950.

Mackie, G. M. *Bible Manners and Customs*. Old Tappan, N.J.: Fleming H. Revell Co., 1984.

Merrill, Selak. *East of the Jordan*. New York: Charles Scribner's Sons, 1883.

Meshorer, Ya'akov. *Coins of the Ancient World*. Minneapolis: Lerner Publications Co., 1975.

_____. *Jewish Coins of the Second Temple Period*. Tel-Aviv: Am Hassefer and Masada, 1967.

Miller, J. Lane & Madeleine S. *Harper's Bible Dictionary*. New York: Harper & Brothers, 1954.

_____. *Harper's Encyclopedia of Bible Life*. San Francisco: Harper & Row, 1971.

Mindlin, Valerie & Cornfeld, Gaalyahu. *The Epic of the Maccabees*. New York: The Macmillan Co., 1962.

Minkin, Jacob S. *Herod*. New York: The Macmillan Co., 1936.

Neil, James. *Everyday Life in the Holy Land*. London: Church Missions to Jews, 1937.

Neil, William, ed. *The Bible Companion*. New York: McGraw-Hill Book Co., 1960.

Nevin, John W. *A Summary of Biblical Antiquities*. Philadelphia: American Sunday-School Union, 1849.

The New English Bible. Cambridge: Oxford Press, 1970.

Nun, Mendel. *Ancient Jewish Fishery*. Hakibbutz Hameuchad Publishing House, 1964.

Packer, James I., etal. eds. *The Bible Almanac*. Carmel, New York: Guideposts, 1980.

Paremelee, Alice. *All the Birds of the Bible*. New York: Harper & Brothers, 1959.

Parish, Elijah. *Sacred Geography of Gazetteer of the Bible*. Boston: Samuel T. Armstrong, 1813.

Parrot, André. *Samaria*. New York: Philosophical Library, 1958.

Paul, Shalom M. and Dever, William G. *Biblical Archaeology*. Jerusalem: Keter Publishing House Jerusalem, 1973.

Perowne, Stewart. *The Life and Times of Herod the Great*. New York: Abingdon Press.

Powell, Frank J. *The Trial of Jesus Christ*. Grand Rapids: Wm. B. Eerdmans Publishing Co., 1954.

Quennel, Marjorie & Quennel, C. H. *Everyday Life in Roman Times*. London: Carousel Books, 1974.

Radin, Max. *The Jews Among the Greeks and Romans*. Philadelphia: The Jewish Publication Society of America, 1915.

Reader's Digest Atlas of the Bible. Pleasantville, N.Y.: The Reader's Digest Association, 1981.

Rice, Edwin Wilbur. *Orientalisms in Bible Lands*. Philadelphia: The American Sunday-School Union, 1910.

Sanger, Richard H. *Where the Jordan Flows*. Washington, D.C.: The Middle East Institute, 1963.

Schürer, Emil. *A History of the Jewish People in the Time of Jesus*. New York: Schocken Books, 1961.

Shanks, Hershel. *Judaism in Stone*. New York: Harper & Row, 1979.

Shaw, J. R. *Background to the New Testament*. London: United Society for Christian Literature, 1961.

Simkins, Michael. *The Roman Army from Caesar to Trojan*. Reading, Berkshire: Osprey Publishing, 1956.

Smith, David. *The Days of His Flesh*. New York: Hodder & Stoughton, 1910.

Smith, George Adam. *The Historical Geography of the Holy Land*. New York: A. C. Armstrong and Son, 1906.

_____. *History of Jerusalem*. Jerusalem: Ariel Publishing Co., Reprint 1907.

Smith, William. *A Dictionary of the Bible*. New York: Fleming H. Revell Co., 1904.

Soares, Theodore Gerald. *The Social Institutions and Ideals of the Bible*. New York: The Abingdon Press, 1915.

Stainer, John. *The Music of the Bible*. London: Cassell, Petter & Galpin.

Stalker, James. *The Trial and Death of Jesus Christ*. New York: American Tract Society, 1903.

Stanley, Arthur Penrhyn. *Sinai and Palestine*. London: John Murray, 1868.

Stapfer, Edmond. *Palestine in the Time of Christ*. New York: A. C. Armstrong and Son, 1885.

Starr, Chester G. *The Ancient Romans*. New York: Oxford University Press, 1971.

Sukenik & Mayer. *The Third Wall*. Jerusalem: Hebrew University Press, 1930.

Sutcliffe, Edmund F. *The Monks of Qumran*. Westminster: The Newman Press, 1960.

Swift, Fletcher H. *Education in Ancient Israel to 70 A. D.* Chicago: The Open Court Publishing Co., 1919.

Tamarin, Alfred H. *Revolt in Judea: The Road to Masada*. New York: Galahad Books, 1968.

Toynbee, Arnold. *The Crucible of Christianity*. New York: World Publishing Co., 1969.

Tristram, H. B. *The Natural History of the Bible*. London: Society for Promoting Christian Knowledge, 1868.

Van Deursen, Arie. *Illustrated Dictionary of Bible Manners and Customs*. New York: Philosophical Library, 1967.

Vermés, Géza. *Discovery in the Judean Desert*. New York: Desclee Company, 1956.

Walker, Winifred. *All the Plants of the Bible*. New York: Harper & Brothers, 1957.

Wallace, Edwin Sherman. *Jerusalem the Holy*. New York: Fleming H. Revell Co., 1898.

Weir, Shelagh. *Spinning and Weaving in Palestine*. London: The British Museum, 1970.

Weiss, G. Christian. *Insights into Bible Times and Customs*. Chicago: Moody Press, 1972.

Whiston, William, tr. *The Works of Flavius Josephus*. Elizabeth, N.J.: E. Sanderson and B. F. Brookfield, 1829.

Wight, Fred H. *Manners and Customs of Bible Lands*. Chicago: Moody Press, 1953.

Wilkinson, John. *Jerusalem as Jesus Knew It*. London: Thames and Hudson, 1978.

Williamson, G. A. *The World of Josephus*. Boston: Little, Brown and Co., 1964.

Wirgin and Mandel. *The History of Coins and Symbols in Ancient Israel*. New York: Exposition Press, 1958.

Wright, G. Ernest. *Biblical Archaeology*. Philadelphia: The Westminster Press, 1957.

Yadin, Yigael. *Masada*. London: Cardinal, 1975.

Publications:
National Geographic Society
Israel Exploration Journal
Biblical Archaeologist
Biblical Archaeology Review

SCRIPTURE INDEX

(Compiled by Wendy Nemic and Paul Simonsen)

SCRIPTURE INDEX